Proper
Healthy
Food

NICK KNOWLES

Proper Healthy Food

Hearty vegan & vegetarian recipes for meat lovers

BOOKS

To my family, who love me even when I'm a pain, make sure I'm grounded between my flights of fancy and would like me to hang around a while. The feeling is mutual.

10 9 8 7 6 5 4 3 2 1

BBC Books, an imprint of Ebury Publishing
20 Vauxhall Bridge Road,
London SW1V 2SA

BBC Books is part of the Penguin Random House
group of companies whose addresses can be
found at global.penguinrandomhouse.com

Penguin
Random House
UK

First published by BBC Books in 2017

www.penguin.co.uk

A CIP catalogue record for this book
is available from the British Library

ISBN 9781785942242

Printed and bound by Firmengruppe APPL,
aprinta druck, Wemding, Germany

Penguin Random House is committed to a
sustainable future for our business, our readers
and our planet. This book is made from Forest
Stewardship Council ® certified paper.

MIX
Paper from
responsible sources
FSC® C018179

Commissioning editor: Lisa Dyer
Editor: Charlotte Macdonald
Design and art direction: Smith & Gilmour
Photographer: Andrew Burton
Food stylist: Philippa Spence and Sian Henley
Prop stylist: Morag Farquhar

CONTENTS

INTRODUCTION

You might have bought this book yourself, or you might have been given it and you're thinking, 'I'm not really a veggie kind of person!'

If you're the latter, that's me a year ago. As I told my wife: 'I'll join in a juicing regime when they start juicing Scotch eggs.'

Let's face it, I'm not vegan- or veggie-shaped, I'm a big unit – pushing 17 stone, 6 foot 2 inches tall and with a 46-inch chest – and I need a wholesome bowl of fuel to keep going. A bowl of salad leaves is not going to work for me. The health benefits of a vegetarian or vegan diet are indisputable – more veg and less meat and dairy means living healthier and sometimes longer, but I do love steak and cheese. Man, I love cheese!

But here's the news: following a veggie diet doesn't mean you have to wear tie-dye trousers that hang around your knees, weave ribbons in your hair or even swear off meat and dairy for ever.

I'm vegan mostly, vegetarian occasionally, and if friends cook me a meal with meat in it I'll eat it because I don't want to be rude and it's a nice change once in a while. And if I'm three pints in at the rugby and smell frying onions, I'll have a cheeseburger and not feel bad because tomorrow and the next day I'll mostly be eating healthily.

So really the message is, don't beat yourself up about it – then there's no wagon to fall off! There's a term for it too – there always is, and normally coming from California: *flexitarian*. In short it means you can eat everything, you just choose to cut down on the things that could do you most harm.

I've always loved preparing food and trying new tastes. I grew up in Southall, in West London, where many of my classmates had parents from India, Pakistan, Sri Lanka, North Africa, the Caribbean and Poland. Every family's food had a different flavour and unusual ingredients; you couldn't call at any house without the mums filling you with delicious grub. Visiting my friends' houses was like a culinary tour of the world, and I think that's where my love of spices and herbs started. It certainly wasn't from my mum, she made big wholesome meals that kept us full, but a sprig of mint in the new potatoes was about as exotic as it got and garlic was the work of the devil.

When I left school I went travelling for a while. I think I wanted to try to see many of the places that my friends' parents had talked about, and of course to see if I could find some of those taste sensations again. To this day I eat my way round the Notting Hill

Carnival every summer – goat curry, salt fish, honey roast plantain... Well, that was the case until a year ago.

I'd reached the point where things had to change. I had lost control of my weight, I was stressed, on the road a lot so I wasn't eating well and I felt like my head was too full to think. Sound familiar?

So I went to a retreat in Thailand. Being there calmed my head and got my eating back in order. I reduced my cholesterol and at the same time my weight. I felt lighter, less sluggish and truly happier inside. I was doing yoga and started working out. All of these lifestyle changes stemmed from me changing my eating habits to a diet of mostly veg and fruit.

It's common sense, really: you're only as healthy as the food you put into your body and we all know deep down that processed food, with its sugars and fats and salts and preservatives, etc., just isn't good for you.

When I got back to Britain I tried to keep going with the diet and lifestyle that I'd adopted in Thailand, but there just wasn't the variety of ingredients available to make it easy to do so. The veggie food that was on offer seemed thin and weedy, but then I remembered the global neighbourhood that I'd lived in while growing up and knew that this boring approach to veggie cooking didn't have to be the case. I knew that in many cultures around the world meat is scarce, so instead they do amazing things with herbs and veg, fruit and spices, and for veggies – eggs and cheeses. If you think about it, there are 70,000 edible plants growing around the world, so surely we should be able to get creative with them like so many other cultures have?

I'm not a chef, but I did want to eat well whilst being vegan/ veggie (mostly), which is why I got to work on these recipes that anyone can prepare. As I've said, you don't have to cut out meat and fish completely; if you eat veggie once a week you'll be healthier, if you do it three times a week you'll be a lot healthier, and if you spend most of your week eating like this, like me you could end up several kilos lighter, with lower cholesterol and more energy for work and family. But I'm sure the more cynical will wonder just how serious I am about all this. Well, I've put my money where my mouth is. I now co-own two vegan restaurants – so you can see I mean what I say.

So, this is the vegan–veggie cook book for meat eaters! Give it a go, have fun, eat hearty and, most importantly, enjoy! If I can do this – so can you.

WHY GO VEGAN OR VEGETARIAN?

Following a vegan or vegetarian diet is very much a personal choice, and there are many varied reasons why people choose this diet – animal welfare, environmental concerns or simply texture and flavour. Whatever your opinion of these arguments, one thing that is indisputable is that there are many health advantages to removing meat and fish from the diet.

First, though, back to basics. Vegan and vegetarian – what's the difference? Well, traditionally, a vegetarian diet is one that eliminates meat, poultry and fish, but usually includes eggs and dairy. A vegan diet goes a step further and rules out all foods that derive from animals in any form, including dairy products, eggs and, for some really strict vegans, honey.

This means that fruit and vegetables form the foundation of any plant-based diet, particularly one followed by vegans, but with such a huge range of both ingredients now available, this needn't be a boring way to eat. Mixing it up on a daily basis and 'eating the rainbow' means plates packed with colour and flavour, which is what this book is all about.

What's the benefit to my health?
Eating a primarily plant-based diet isn't all about aesthetics and keeping it interesting, fruit and veg are also very rich in nutrients, and the various colours represent different antioxidants and phyto-chemicals, including anthocyanins, flavonoids and carotenoids. These compounds protect against modern-day diseases, but each in a slightly different way, which is why we need to eat a good selection of them.

Following a vegan diet with a greater quantity of fruit and veg is also thought to help reduce the risk of certain cancers. Limiting the intake of animal-based foods, including dairy, in addition to following the other recommended dietary advice – such as reducing the amount of refined sugars, salt, hydrogenated and saturated fats you eat – also reduces your risk.

Most vegetarians base their diets on cereals, pulses, nuts, seeds – in addition to fruit and vegetables – to make sure they can get all the essential nutrients that their bodies require. Vegans, of course, have to eat a more diverse range of foods to compensate for their more restrictive diet. However, this is not a disadvantage – quite the reverse, there is much evidence to support the idea that people following a vegan, or mostly vegan, diet enjoy a lower Body Mass Index (BMI), which contributes to better general health. In addition, their markers for heart disease and type 2 diabetes, two of the most common modern-day diseases, are improved with lower serum cholesterol, reduced blood sugar levels and lower blood pressure because of their diet.

Specifically, these health benefits are thanks to the high fibre content of the diet, and the fact that vegans have higher intakes of vitamin B6 and folate than their meat-eating counterparts. What's more, vegan diets are lower in calories, have a lower glycaemic load, are richer in protective phytochemicals and lower in fat, with a preference towards the healthier unsaturated variety.

Whole grains and legumes are another cornerstone of a vegan diet; their inclusion improves blood sugar control by slowing the rate of carbohydrate absorption and cutting your risk of diabetes.

What might you be missing out on?
Although a plant-based diet has clear advantages, eliminating all animal foods does increase the likelihood of some nutritional shortfalls, notably protein and some essential minerals. In order to ensure a balanced and healthy diet, these nutrients must be sought elsewhere.

On average, vegans eat less protein than meat-eaters, but whole grains and legumes are key sources of protein, so diets should include lentils, peas, soy and beans as well as quinoa to help maintain a sufficient intake.

In addition to protein, of most concern for this way of eating is making sure the daily diet includes vitamins B12 and D, calcium, as well as the long chain omega-3 fats. In some cases iron and zinc levels may also be low because they're less absorbable from plant foods. If you don't include animal-derived foods you may need to consider supplementation, or at the very least including appropriate fortified foods. For example, only a few leafy greens have high levels of absorbable calcium – good inclusions are kale, cabbage and watercress – but if you, as a vegan, are not eating 2–3 portions of these a day then you need to include calcium-fortified foods such as plant milk or tofu, or consider taking a supplement.

Following a flexible approach to a plant-based diet like Nick's can be beneficial in making sure you are eating a healthy, balanced diet and ensures that you are not missing out on any important nutrients. Of course, cooking from scratch is an ideal way to monitor your intake of all healthy – and unhealthy – ingredients and means you know exactly what you are putting into your body.

So, whatever your reasons for following a vegan or vegetarian diet, armed with this book you can be sure of a healthy, happy you.

NICK'S STORECUPBOARD

With the right ingredients in your cupboards you can turn any bunch of vegetables into something yummy. Here's what I always keep handy.

Herbs, spices and seasoning
Spices – cumin, coriander, chilli flakes, curry powder, cinnamon, nutmeg, mustard powder, sweet paprika, cayenne pepper, turmeric and saffron.

Herbs – oregano, thyme, rosemary, sage, basil, parsley, dill and chives.

Seasonings – garlic, ginger (ground and fresh), lemons, limes, salt and pepper, fresh red and green chillies, mustard (English, Dijon, wholegrain), miso paste, vegetable stock cubes, Marmite or Vegemite.

Sauces
My essentials are Tabasco, Worcestershire, soy, sriracha and fish sauce. Do note that Worcestershire, oyster and fish sauces are all made with fish and seafood essences, so are not vegetarian/vegan. A good deli will find you vegan versions of most sauces and a quick search on the Internet will help you out.

Nuts
Cashews, peanuts, pecans, almonds and hazelnuts.

Oils
Extra virgin olive, coconut, rapeseed, truffle-infused olive and sesame oil.

Seeds
Sesame, salted pumpkin, sunflower and poppy seeds.

Sweeteners
Maple syrup, Medjool dates, honey for the veggies not the vegans. Black treacle is a good substitute for honey whenever I've suggested it in a recipe.

Dairy
Milk – for vegans replace milk with soya, almond or coconut milk. I tend to use coconut in sweet dishes, pancakes and sweet pastries, and almond in savoury as I'm not fond of soy. Other vegan milks will work too – you have to decide for yourself which works for you.

Yoghurt – try coconut-based, non-dairy yoghurt for the vegans.

Cheese – vegan cheese is difficult as they haven't really cracked it yet but I'll say this – there are some good vegan Parmesan alternatives for pesto or for sprinkling over pasta.

Nutritional yeast

The vegan's friend, adding a cheesy tang to many dishes and sauces. It goes well with tahini for sauces by the way, and it's healthy too, providing nutrition but low in calories. Good on vitamins, in particular B-complex (check the tin – not all do), it contains folates, thiamine, riboflavin, niacin, selenium and zinc, making it a great all-round superfood!

Meat substitutes

I use tofu sparingly as any soya product can be fattening. Seitan is a wheat-based product, so not so good for those intolerant. Try vegetarian sausages too.

Eggs

An egg yolk substitute in all recipes where yolks are used to bind is lecithin. It's good for you, you can get it in dried granule form from most health food shops and one tablespoon equals one egg yolk. Also, rather than heightening cholesterol it actually helps reduce it.

Pickles

I'm a big pickle eater, and I'm not giving them up despite being quite high in sugars. We'll do healthier pickling next book. In the meantime fermented foods are better – so try sauerkraut instead or kimchi, which is a Taiwanese fermented veg pickle kind of thing. Good for you and yummy.

Key veggie ingredients

Veg – mushrooms (wild, button, portobello, flat, chicken of the woods mushrooms if you can get them), tomatoes (vine, cherry, chopped and passata), avocados, sweet potatoes, peppers, butternut squash, artichokes and aubergines.

Others – sage and onion stuffing, lentils (green, puy), beans (black, cannellini, borlotti and mixed dried beans are always handy), chickpeas, chestnuts, breadcrumbs, polenta, pearl barley, couscous, olives and chickpea flour.

ONE
BANGING
BREAKFASTS

RED PEPPER SHAKSHUKA

2 tbsp olive oil
1 red chilli, deseeded
   and finely chopped
1 onion, finely chopped
3 medium red peppers,
   deseeded and sliced
   into thin strips
4 garlic cloves,
   roughly chopped
1 tsp ground cumin
1 tsp turmeric
A pinch of saffron
400g chopped tomatoes
3 medium eggs

TO SERVE
4 tbsp natural yoghurt
2 tbsp flat-leaf parsley,
   roughly chopped,
   to garnish

Over the years I've been to Dubai, Qatar and Abu Dhabi and eaten quite a lot of Arabic food, but it was only recently while I was eating in an Arabic restaurant in Thailand of all places, that I found out how much Arabic food is vegan or veggie. This shakshuka is exotic, filling when served with crusty bread, and looks the bomb when you cook it for others.

1 Heat the oil in a deep frying pan until hot and add the red chilli and chopped onion. Sizzle for 2-3 minutes until the onion has begun to soften. Add the sliced peppers, garlic and spices. Keep up the heat and continue to fry, covered, for 10-12 minutes. You want the peppers to be soft but not to char.

2 Pour in the tin of tomatoes and continue to simmer for a further 8 minutes, uncovered, until the mixture has thickened slightly.

3 Using a spoon shape 3 slight 'holes' in your pepper mixture. Crack eggs into these holes – it doesn't matter if the white seeps onto the surface of the mixture. Cover and cook until the yolks are just set, about 10 minutes.

4 Serve with yoghurt and parsley.

ALL-DAY BREAKFAST OMELETTE

1 tbsp olive oil
3 chestnut or portobellini
   mushrooms, wiped and sliced
6 whole cherry tomatoes
2 large handfuls of baby spinach
50g Cheddar cheese, grated
4 large eggs, lightly whisked
1 tbsp milk
4 tbsp ricotta cheese
1 tbsp fresh thyme leaves
Salt and freshly ground
   black pepper

Eggs. Definitely the toughest thing for me to give up on the vegan trail, as well as cheese. So when I'm feeling the call of the omelette, this is my go-to recipe. To make it extra light, whisk the eggs until they're all bubbly and full of air.

If you can't get your omelette under the grill, just stick a lid or plate over the pan while you cook it on the hob.

1 Heat the oil in a small ovenproof frying pan, add the mushrooms and tomatoes and fry gently for 5 minutes, then add the spinach and cook for a further 2 minutes.

2 In a medium bowl, whisk together the Cheddar, eggs and milk. Season to taste.

3 Pour the egg mixture over the veg, dot over nuggets of the ricotta, sprinkle over the thyme and cook over a low–medium heat for 5 minutes. Transfer to a grill heated to medium–high and cook for a further 2–3 minutes or until the top of the omelette is just cooked, with a slight wobble. Serve immediately, out of the pan.

APPLE & CINNAMON PORRIDGE

3 tbsp maple syrup
A pinch of ground cinnamon,
    plus extra to serve (optional)
A pinch of ground nutmeg
4 firm crisp apples, cored and
    cut into 1.5–2cm cubes
1 tbsp unsalted butter
700ml water
90g rolled oats
A pinch of salt

Every time I've interviewed a bloke who's made it to 100 he says the secret is 'never argue with the wife and eat porridge'. The Scots' way is to make porridge with water, a sprinkle of salt and a dram of whisky (not before driving!), but here's a sweeter version. By the way, for us big kids a spoonful of raw chocolate powder (ask in your local health shop) and splash of maple syrup makes a more healthy chocolate porridge that even the kids will love.

1 Preheat the oven to 190°C/fan 170°C/gas 5. Line a rimmed baking sheet with baking parchment or tin foil.

2 In a small bowl, combine the maple syrup, cinnamon and nutmeg. Add the apples and toss well to combine. Spread out the apples in a single layer. Break apart the butter and scatter small pieces over the apples. Bake for 15–20 minutes or until the fruit is tender.

3 Meanwhile, pour the water into a small saucepan and place over a moderate heat. Tip in the oats and add the salt. Continue to stir until the porridge has bubbled for 5 minutes or so. Spoon into pre-warmed bowls. Serve topped with the hot roasted apples and a further sprinkling of cinnamon, if you like.

THE BIG BREAKFAST

4 large flat mushrooms,
   wiped and thickly sliced
150g halloumi cheese, sliced
2 tbsp olive oil
1 tsp dried oregano
200g cherry vine tomatoes
2 large eggs
150g baby spinach
A small grating of fresh nutmeg
Salt and freshly ground
   black pepper

I like the ceremony of a big breakfast. It's the best, largest feed of the day so it's got to be wholesome and chunky, even without the bacon and sausage. It's also got to be filling to keep me going all through my morning. Here's my favourite version of the classic big brekkie.

1 Preheat the oven to 180°C/fan 160°C/gas 4. In a large roasting tin, toss together the mushrooms, halloumi, oil and oregano. Season well with salt and a good grind of black pepper and roast in the oven for 10 minutes. Remove the tin from the oven, toss the mushrooms, add the stem of vine tomatoes and roast for a further 10 minutes or until the halloumi is slightly caramelised.

2 Bring a large, deep pan of lightly salted water to the boil. Once boiling, lower the heat a little and swirl the water with the handle of a wooden spoon to create a whirlpool. Once the whirlpool had almost completely subsided, crack an egg into it and cook it for 3 minutes. Remove the egg with a slotted spoon and transfer to a plate lined with kitchen paper, then repeat with the second egg.

3 Place a small saucepan over a medium heat, add the spinach and ½ tablespoon of water. Cover the pan and cook for 3 minutes or until wilted, then stir through a little nutmeg and season to taste.

4 Spoon the roasted tomatoes, mushrooms and halloumi onto individual plates, top each with some of the spinach and a soft poached egg along with a good grind of salt and pepper, then serve while piping hot.

VEGETARIAN
PREP TIME: 30 MINUTES
+ 30 MINUTES RESTING
COOKING TIME: 30 MINUTES
SERVES 6

GALETTES WITH EGGS, GARLIC MUSHROOMS & SPINACH

FOR THE GALETTES
250g plain flour
½ tsp salt
2 large eggs
400ml milk
30g unsalted butter, melted
3 tbsp sunflower oil

FOR THE FILLING
40g unsalted butter
300g chestnut mushrooms,
    sliced
1 small garlic clove, crushed
½ small bunch of chives,
    chopped
300g baby spinach
Zest and a little of the juice
    of 1 lemon
3–4 tbsp mascarpone
Salt and freshly ground
    black pepper

TO SERVE
4 tbsp sunflower oil
6 large eggs

A galette is a posh pancake – you can also use chickpea flour if you prefer, although it tends to break more easily when you flip the pancake.
This is really tasty; I had this almost every lunchtime when I was in Thailand.

1 First make the galette batter. Place the flour and salt into a large mixing bowl, make a well in the centre and crack in the eggs. Whisk in the milk in several additions until you have a smooth and creamy batter. Stir through the melted butter and set aside in the fridge for 30 minutes to rest.

2 Meanwhile, make the filling. Heat the butter in a medium frying pan over a medium heat. Once foaming, add the mushrooms and cook gently for 6 minutes. Add the garlic and cook for a further 2 minutes. Season to taste and stir through the chopped chives.

3 Place the spinach and ½ tablespoon of water into a small pan over a medium heat. Cover and cook for 5 minutes or until wilted. Squeeze away any excess water and pour off. Stir through the lemon zest and a small squeeze of the juice as well as the mascarpone and season well with salt and pepper.

4 To cook the galettes, heat a little of the sunflower oil in a large non-stick frying pan. Add a ladleful of the batter, swirl around the pan and cook over a medium heat for 1 minute. Flip over and finish the other side

for 30 seconds. They should be a deep golden brown colour. Repeat until you have used all of the mixture. Set aside on a plate, cover with foil and keep warm in a low oven.

5 Heat the remaining sunflower oil in a large non-stick frying pan over a low heat. Crack 2 of the 6 eggs into the pan, raise the heat slightly and cook for 3–4 minutes, basting the yolk in a little of the hot oil until the white is cooked and the yolk is still soft and runny. Repeat until all the eggs are cooked.

6 Gently reheat the mushroom and spinach filling in the same pan over a medium heat. Combine the two well and check the seasoning. Spoon the creamy filling into the centre of each galette and pull the four sides inwards to create an open parcel. Top the centre with the fried egg and a little more black pepper. Serve.

VEGETARIAN
PREP TIME: 10 MINUTES
COOKING TIME: 15 MINUTES
SERVES 4 (MAKES 12 PANCAKES)

AMERICAN BLUEBERRY PANCAKES WITH CINNAMON YOGHURT

FOR THE PANCAKES
3 medium eggs
120ml milk
120g plain flour
1½ tsp baking powder
2 tsp caster sugar
Pinch of salt
1 tsp vegetable oil
Small handful of fresh
   blueberries, plus about
   60g extra to serve

**FOR THE CINNAMON
   YOGHURT**
1 tbsp runny honey
¼ tsp ground cinnamon
200g thick Greek-style
   natural yoghurt

Everyone likes a pancake and most people like cinnamon, but not everyone. If you are someone who doesn't, skip the cinnamon and drop a little maple syrup into the yoghurt for a real treat.

1 Separate the eggs into 2 bowls – yolks in one, whites in another. Add the milk, flour, baking powder, sugar and salt to the yolks and whisk together to form a smooth batter.

2 Whisk the egg whites (using an electric whisk) until they form soft peaks – they should be white and voluminous but not too stiff. Fold the whites into the batter with a large spoon, trying to keep as much air in as possible, then transfer the mixture to a large jug.

3 To make the cinnamon yoghurt, simply mix together the honey, cinnamon and yoghurt in a bowl.

4 Gently heat the oil in a large frying pan and wipe out the excess with kitchen paper. Pour circles of the batter, roughly 6cm across, into the pan – you will probably need to do these in batches depending on the size of your pan. Place a few blueberries on top of each one and cook over a medium heat until bubbles appear in the centre of each pancake. Lift the edge of each pancake to look underneath – they should be golden brown. Then flip and cook on the other side for another 2 minutes. Keep the cooked pancakes warm while you cook the rest.

5 Serve the pancakes with a dollop of the cinnamon yoghurt and extra blueberries.

VEGAN
PREP TIME: 10 MINUTES
+ OVERNIGHT SOAKING
NO COOKING TIME
SERVES 4

BIRCHER MUESLI WITH MAPLE, PLUM & PECAN

200g porridge oats
250ml almond milk
250ml apple juice
100g plump raisins
4 ripe plums, destoned
   and sliced
80g pecan nuts,
   roughly chopped
Ground cinnamon,
   for dusting
4 tbsp maple syrup

'The trouble with veggie stuff is it's all rabbit food.' That's the often-heard refrain of those that haven't tried good vegetarian food. Trust me, if the bunny is eating this it's got the better end of the deal.

1 Empty the oats, almond milk and apple juice into a small bowl and mix well. Cover and leave in the fridge overnight.

2 When ready to serve, remove the Bircher muesli from the fridge and spoon into bowls. Top with raisins, slices of plum, chopped pecan nuts, a dusting of cinnamon and a drizzle of maple syrup. Serve immediately.

TIP
The Bircher muesli can be kept in the fridge for up to 3 days.

BLUEBERRY, OAT & BANANA BREAKFAST BARS

150g unsalted butter,
  plus extra for greasing
2 tbsp runny honey
2 tbsp maple syrup
130g caster sugar
2 tsp vanilla extract
300g rolled oats
30g sesame seeds
70g flaked almonds
75g almond butter or
  peanut butter
3 ripe bananas
170g blueberries

There's not always time to make breakfast in the morning, so when you've got a bit longer – maybe at the weekend – make up a batch of these so you can grab one to eat on the way to work or have as a treat in your lunchbox.

1 Preheat the oven to 170°C/fan 150°C/gas 3. Grease a 25 x 25cm traybake tin with butter and line with baking parchment.

2 Into a saucepan, measure the butter, honey, maple syrup, sugar and vanilla, then melt them together over a low heat.

3 While the butter mix is melting, combine the oats, sesame seeds, flaked almonds and nut butter in a large bowl.

4 Peel and mash the bananas in a small bowl with a fork, then add to the oat bowl along with the melted butter mix and, lastly, the blueberries. Give everything a good stir, then tip into the traybake tin and bake in the oven for 25–30 minutes until golden. Allow to cool in the tin for 1–2 hours before slicing into 16 bars.

VEGETARIAN
PREP TIME: 20 MINUTES
COOKING TIME: 20 MINUTES
SERVES 4

REFRIED BEANS ON TOAST WITH AVOCADO & POACHED EGG

2 tbsp olive oil, plus extra
   for the bread
1 small onion, finely diced
1 small bunch of thyme
1 red chilli, finely chopped,
   seeds in
1 garlic clove, crushed
1 tsp ground cumin
1 tsp ground coriander
½ tsp smoked sweet paprika
400g tin black beans, drained
   and rinsed
1 tsp runny honey
Small bunch of fresh coriander,
   stalks and leaves, finely
   chopped, plus extra
   for serving
2 thick slices sourdough bread
2 ripe avocados
Juice of 1 lime
2 tbsp white wine vinegar
4 medium eggs
Salt and freshly ground
   black pepper

Avocado on sourdough toast is great with a few salted pumpkin seeds. This is chunkier with the refried beans and if you're not sure about the beans or the spices, use a tin of baked beans and just keep it chugging away until the sauce has gone super thick. It's proper filling.

1 Heat the olive oil in a large saucepan over a low heat and add in the onion, cook for 8–10 minutes until soft and translucent. Stir through the thyme and chilli and continue to cook for another 2 minutes.

2 Add in the garlic and spices and cook for a further minute. Pour in the beans and let them sauté for 2 minutes until warmed through. Remove the stems of thyme and add 5 tablespoons cold water to the pan. Using a stick blender, pulse the mix until it is soft but retains some texture. Taste and season with the honey, salt and pepper. Add the fresh coriander and set aside.

3 Toast the bread and drizzle generously with olive oil. Halve the avocados, remove the stones and neatly scrape out the flesh whole with a spoon. Slice into lengths and squeeze the lime juice over to prevent the avocados turning brown.

4 Bring a large pan of water to a very gentle simmer. Stir in 1 teaspoon salt and the white wine vinegar. Stir the water vigorously and crack the eggs into the centre one at a time. Let them cook for around 2–3 minutes until the whites are set but the yolk still runny. Remove using a slotted spoon and keep on a plate until needed.

5 To serve, spread a large spoonful of the beans onto half a piece of toast each, topping each with avocado slices, an egg and a sprinkle of fresh coriander.

VEGETARIAN
PREP TIME: 25 MINUTES
COOKING TIME: 35 MINUTES
SERVES 4

BUBBLE & SQUEAK WITH CRISPY FRIED EGG

FOR THE BUBBLE AND SQUEAK

740g (about 3 large) floury potatoes, peeled and cut into large chunks
60g unsalted butter
2 tbsp olive oil
1 medium onion, finely diced
½ head Savoy cabbage, shredded
1 medium egg
¼ whole nutmeg, freshly grated
6 thyme sprigs, leaves picked
2 tbsp plain flour, for dusting

FOR THE FRIED EGGS

2 tbsp sunflower oil
4 medium eggs
Flat-leaf parsley, roughly chopped, to serve
Freshly ground black pepper, to serve

Who doesn't like bubble and squeak? I used to have it with corned beef hash when I was regularly eating meat, but it works fantastically with fried eggs or tomatoes instead. You could also eat it with ketchup – and while there's nothing wrong with that, it really should be brown sauce. I'm just saying, not judging.

1 Boil a large pan of salted water and cook the potatoes for 8–10 minutes until they are soft and break apart easily. Drain and let them cool slightly in the colander.

2 In a wide frying pan, heat half the butter, 1 tablespoon of olive oil and add the onion. Cook over a very low heat for 8–10 minutes until soft and translucent. Add in the shredded cabbage and 90ml water and sauté for another 6–7 minutes over a high heat. Stir regularly until wilted and tender, then set aside.

3 In a large bowl, crush the potatoes with a fork and leave to cool slightly before adding in the cabbage, egg, nutmeg and thyme. Mix everything together well and then dust your hands with the flour. Shape the mix into 8 patties, each about 2.5cm deep and 7cm round.

4 In the same pan used for the cabbage, melt the remaining butter and olive oil over a medium heat. Fry the bubble and squeak cakes for 3 minutes on each side until golden and crispy. Remove to a baking tray and keep warm in an oven at 150°C/fan 130°C/gas 2.

5 Next, heat the sunflower oil in a frying pan and crack in 4 eggs. Fry over a high heat for 2 minutes until crisp and brown around the edges with the yolk still runny. Serve on top of the bubble and squeak cakes (2 per person). Garnish with chopped parsley and pepper.

VEGETARIAN
PREP TIME: 5 MINUTES
COOKING TIME: 10 MINUTES
SERVES 4

PARMESAN CHILLI SCRAMBLED EGGS

8 medium eggs
A knob of butter
A pinch of chilli flakes
1–2 tbsp chopped coriander
Salt and freshly ground
    black pepper
Hot buttered toast, to serve
2 tbsp finely grated Parmesan
    cheese, to serve

Once you've mastered scrambled eggs – and the trick is to take the pan off the heat just before the eggs have set so they are not too dry – you can add pretty much anything you like, such as chopped spring onions, herbs or tomatoes. This version is one of my favourites.

1 Crack the eggs in a small bowl and gently beat with a wooden spoon.

2 Put a saucepan over a medium–low heat and melt the butter. Add the chilli flakes and allow them to sizzle for a few seconds before pouring in the eggs. Stir slowly with a wooden spoon. Keep stirring until the eggs begin to set, 4–6 minutes, but remove the pan from the heat just before serving (they will continue to cook a little even after they are off the heat).

3 Fold through the chopped coriander and some salt and pepper to taste. Serve over hot buttered toast with a sprinkling of Parmesan.

MAKE IT VEGAN
There's a good vegan Parmesan out there and a tofu scramble, too, that's better than you'd expect.

VEGETARIAN
PREP TIME: 15 MINUTES
COOKING TIME: 45 MINUTES
MAKES 1 LOAF

SEEDY CHEESY SODA BREAD

45g butter, cubed,
 plus extra for greasing
500g white bread flour,
 plus extra for dusting
2 tsp bicarbonate of soda
1 tsp salt
1 tsp caster sugar
45g Parmesan cheese,
 finely grated
100g mature Cheddar
 cheese, grated
290–350ml buttermilk
Milk, for the dough (optional)
 and for brushing
30g pumpkin seeds

Use your loaf and make your own bread. No, I'm not joking and don't you immediately page on. You can do this and people will look at you with new eyes – and the smell of baking bread beats any air freshener in your house. Proper chunky, cheesy bread.

1 Preheat the oven to 190°C/fan 170°C/gas 5. Grease a baking sheet.

2 Sift the flour and bicarbonate of soda into a large mixing bowl and stir in the salt, sugar and Parmesan and Cheddar. Rub the butter into the flour using your fingertips. Make a well in the centre and pour in the buttermilk, stirring as you go. If necessary, add a tablespoon or two of milk to bring the mixture together; it should form a soft dough, just this side of sticky.

3 Shape into a round and, using a floured handle of a wooden spoon, create a cross on the surface by pushing the wooden handle roughly halfway down into your uncooked loaf. Repeat to make a cross shape. Brush the loaf with milk and sprinkle with pumpkin seeds.

4 Bake for 45 minutes until the bread is cooked through. Allow to cool slightly before serving in slices.

BOSTON BAKED BEANS

500g dried white beans or
   tinned cannellini beans,
   drained and rinsed
1 large onion, cut in half
2 fresh bay leaves
4 peppercorns
100ml maple syrup
100g brown sugar
2 tbsp ketchup
½ tbsp chilli flakes
1 tsp salt
1 tbsp Worcestershire sauce
1 tbsp Dijon mustard
Salt and freshly ground
   black pepper

**This is baked beans on…on…erm…hyped up!
Sweet, savoury, sticky and just the bomb – big boys'
baked beans. Make a big pan of them before your
mates come round for the sport and ladle onto thick
sourdough toast.**

1 Put the beans, onion, bay leaves and peppercorns
in a large 2-litre pot and cover with 1.5 litres of cold
water. Simmer, uncovered, for about 1 hour or until the
beans are tender. Drain the beans but keep 900ml of
the cooking water. Remove and discard the halved
onion and bay leaves.

2 In the now-empty pot, add the maple syrup, brown
sugar, ketchup, chilli flakes, salt, Worcestershire sauce
and Dijon mustard and 600ml of the reserved cooking
liquid. Bring to a simmer and cook over a medium heat
for a few minutes until the sauce has come together.

3 Add the beans to the sauce and leave to cook on
a low heat for 5–6 hours, stirring occasionally and
topping up with cold water if the pot becomes too
dry. Cook until the beans are tender and the sauce
has become syrupy. Season to taste and serve.

CARIBBEAN BUCKWHEAT GRANOLA

300g buckwheat
250g rolled oats
3 tbsp sesame seeds
4 tbsp coconut oil
4 tbsp clear runny honey
½ tsp fine sea salt
1 tsp ground cinnamon
A little grated nutmeg
60g dried mango, chopped
60g coconut flakes
60g banana chips, broken

Why would you bother making your own granola when they sell boxes of it ready made? Well, it's cheaper, tastier, you can go heavy on your favourite ingredient instead of searching for the only bit of pineapple, and there are no hidden sugars, colours or preservatives either.

1 Preheat the oven to 180°C/fan 160°C/gas 4.

2 Tip the buckwheat, oats and sesame seeds into a large mixing bowl. In a small saucepan melt the coconut oil and honey together. Tip the liquid into the oat mixture and mix with the sea salt, cinnamon, nutmeg, mango, coconut flakes and banana chips.

3 Line 2 large baking sheets with non-stick baking parchment and spread the mixture out on the sheets in an even layer, then place in the oven and cook for 15–20 minutes. After that time, break up the granola, shake it around and pop it back in the oven for a further 10 minutes or until golden brown and crunchy.

4 Leave the mixture to cool completely, then break it into bite-sized pieces. It will keep in an airtight container for up to 2 weeks.

TWO
THE BIG
LUNCH BOX

SWEET POTATO & GOOEY CHEDDAR CHEESE MUFFINS

500g sweet potatoes,
  peeled and grated
3 tbsp veg oil
3 tsp wholegrain mustard
150g mature Cheddar cheese,
  half grated and half
  roughly chopped
2 tbsp chives, chopped
5 large eggs, lightly whisked
2 tbsp yoghurt
240g wholemeal self-raising
  flour
½ tsp salt
A pinch of freshly ground
  black pepper
3 tbsp pumpkin or
  sunflower seeds

Sweet potatoes are the food of sports champions – it's the protein–carb combo of choice for top rugby players. Ok, we are adding Cheddar and we are talking about a muffin, but I think we can say that this is therefore a sports cake? No? Ok, it's just tasty with a coffee.

1 Line an 8 hole muffin tray with muffin cases and preheat the oven to 180°C/fan 160°C/gas 4.

2 In a large bowl mix together the sweet potatoes, oil, 50g of the Cheddar, chives, eggs and yoghurt. Stir through the flour, salt and pepper. Spoon the mixture in to the cases and top each one with the remaining cheese and pumpkin seeds. Bake in the middle of the oven for 55 minutes–1 hour or until a skewer comes out clean. Once cooked, set aside on a cooling rack to cool down slightly. Split open and eat warm whilst the cheese is still hot and gooey.

SWEET VEGETABLE & CHEDDAR PASTIES

FOR THE FILLING

2 large white potatoes, peeled and cut into 1–1.5cm cubes
2 sweet potatoes, peeled and cut into 1–1.5cm cubes
1 large carrot, peeled and finely chopped into 1–1.5cm cubes
150g swede, peeled and cut into 1–1.5cm cubes
6 spring onions, finely sliced
3 tbsp melted unsalted butter
2 thyme sprigs, leaves only
75g mature Cheddar cheese
1 tsp freshly ground black pepper
½ tsp sea salt

FOR THE PASTRY

500g plain flour
1 tsp salt
250g cold unsalted butter, diced
1 large egg, lightly beaten
2 tbsp poppy seeds

Now there's no reason why a veg pastie can't be as good as a standard Cornish one. You can add veggie mince to this if you want, but to be honest a pastie is all about the swede, carrot, potato and pepper anyway. If should be peppery as you like and freshly ground pepper is always best to get the aroma.

1 Bring a large pan of lightly salted water to the boil. Add both types of potato, the carrot and swede and boil rapidly for 6–7 minutes, until just soft. Strain the vegetables and mash slightly, just enough so they still retain their texture, and set aside.

2 Make the pastry. Sift the flour and salt into a large mixing bowl. Add the butter to the dry mixture and rub together using your fingertips to make a slightly lumpy crumb. Rapidly stir through 6 tablespoons of cold water, then add another ½ tablespoon if it looks too dry. Bring together with your hands. Divide into 4 flat pucks. Wrap each one in cling film and chill for 15 minutes.

3 Mix the mashed vegetables together with the spring onions, melted butter, thyme, Cheddar and black pepper. Season with a little sea salt.

4 Preheat the oven to 180°C/fan 160°C/gas 4. Roll out each pastry round to about 22cm, then spoon a quarter of the filling into one half of a pastry round. Brush a little beaten egg along the border and fold the pastry over the filling to seal. Crimp the sealed edge with a fork. Repeat with the other three pastry rounds and brush with the remaining egg. Sprinkle over the poppy seeds and transfer to a baking sheet lined with non-stick baking parchment. Bake for 45–50 minutes or until golden brown. Serve warm.

BIG GREEN FRITTATA

2 medium courgettes, sliced
    into 0.5–1cm rounds
100g fine green beans, topped
    but the 'tails' left intact
11 medium eggs, lightly beaten
2 tbsp basil, finely chopped
2 tbsp flat-leaf parsley, finely
    chopped
1 tbsp chives, finely chopped
1 tbsp dill, finely chopped
35g Grana Padano cheese,
    grated
¼ whole nutmeg, grated
2 tbsp whole milk
1 tbsp olive oil
230g frozen peas, thawed
Salt and freshly ground
    black pepper

Another big hearty feed. You need to blanch the beans for this but sometimes I'll griddle the courgette first rather than boil it, to lose some water. Also, you can swap the Grana Padano for Cheddar, if you prefer, or even Parmesan.

1 Preheat the oven to 160°C/fan 140°C/gas 3.

2 Bring a medium saucepan of water to the boil and cook the courgettes and green beans for 3–4 minutes until just al dente. Drain well, run under cold water to stop the cooking process and set aside.

3 In a large bowl, whisk together the eggs, all the herbs, Grana Padano cheese, nutmeg, milk, salt and pepper. Preheat the grill to High.

4 Using a pastry brush or kitchen paper, coat a deep, 28cm ovenproof frying pan with oil, ensuring the sides are well greased. Set the pan over a medium heat, then pour in the herby egg mixture. Add the peas, blanched courgettes and green beans to the wet frittata in the pan, spreading them out evenly and allowing some to protrude above the surface of the egg.

5 Reduce the heat to medium–low and leave the frittata to gently cook, without stirring, until the egg is just setting but the centre is still soft, 14–16 minutes. Move the pan to the grill and cook the top of the frittata for a few minutes, until it's puffed and slightly golden. Leave it to sit for 5 minutes before sliding it out of the pan onto a plate or chopping board and serving.

QUICK FLAKY PASTRY PIZZA

Flour, for dusting
500g block puff pastry
200ml passata
150g mozzarella, torn
　　into chunks
70g pitted black olives
½ bunch of basil leaves, torn
Salt and freshly ground
　　black pepper

TO SERVE
1 garlic clove, crushed
2 tbsp olive oil

So this is the first vegetarian thing you should try probably – it's so easy. You can buy the pastry ready made on a roll or in a block, just look in the chiller cabinet at the supermarket. With the roll you won't even need a rolling pin, just make a square pizza by unrolling the pastry onto a baking tray. (If you haven't got a rolling pin, try using a wine bottle, it does the trick!) This quick pizza is great for the kids and for a carpet picnic.

1 Preheat the oven to 200°C/fan 180°C/gas 6. Lightly dust a work surface with a little flour. Roll the pastry into a round, roughly 25–28cm wide. Slide the rolled-out pastry onto a floured, flat baking sheet and prick all over the base with a fork. Bake in the oven for 15–20 minutes, until slightly browned.

2 Remove from the oven and dollop over the passata. Dot with the mozzarella and olives and return to the oven for a further 10–12 minutes. Remove from the oven and finish with the basil, salt and a grind of black pepper. Stir the crushed garlic into the oil, and just before serving, drizzle the oil over the pizza, slice up and serve.

CHUNKY CHICKPEA, HALLOUMI & SWEETCORN BURGERS

FOR THE PATTIES
2 tbsp olive oil
1 small onion, finely chopped
1 small garlic clove, crushed
1 tsp ground coriander
2 tbsp parsley, roughly chopped,
   plus extra to garnish
400g tin chickpeas,
   drained and rinsed
200g tinned sweetcorn
   (drained weight)
100g plain flour
50g strong smoked
   Cheddar cheese, grated
50g dried breadcrumbs
1 medium egg yolk
A sprinkle of paprika

FOR THE BURGERS
2 banana shallots, quartered
4 portobello mushrooms,
   deskinned
3 tbsp vegetable oil,
   plus extra for frying
100g cherry vine tomatoes
4 slices halloumi cheese
4 soft brioche rolls
2 tbsp good-quality
   mayonnaise
Salt and freshly ground
   black pepper

I couldn't do this book without a big chunky burger, so here it is. It's on the front of the book for a reason! This veggie burger has got to be filling and a proper manwich. Sometimes I make sage and onion stuffing flat patties to go into it, too, but this is big enough to start with. Serve with my Smoky Sweet Potato Fries (page 149).

1 Heat the oil in a medium non-stick frying pan over a medium–low heat. Add the onion, garlic, ground coriander and a good pinch of salt, then fry gently for 6–8 minutes or until soft and translucent. Remove from the heat and allow to cool a little.

2 Place the parsley (leaves and stalks), chickpeas, sweetcorn and 60g of the flour into the large bowl of a food processor. Blitz several times to make a rough-textured paste. Tip into a large mixing bowl and combine with the softened onions, Cheddar, breadcrumbs and egg yolk. Season really well. Form the mixture into 4 thick patties, place on a tray lined with non-stick baking parchment and pop in the fridge for 30–40 minutes to firm up.

3 Preheat the oven to 200°C/fan 180°C/gas 6. Place the shallots and whole mushrooms in a roasting dish, drizzle with oil, season and roast for 10 minutes. Add the vine tomatoes and roast for a further 5 minutes. Remove from the oven, sprinkle with salt and set aside.

4 Meanwhile, cook the patties. Mix the remaining flour with the paprika and coat each 'burger' in a little of the flavoured flour. Heat some oil and fry the patties, over a medium–high heat, for 5–6 minutes on each side until golden. Transfer to the hot oven and continue to cook for a further 12–14 minutes until cooked through.

5 Add the halloumi slices to the frying pan and gently fry for 2–3 minutes, turning halfway through cooking. Split each bun open, top with a veggie burger, a slice of halloumi, mushroom, a dollop of mayonnaise and a cluster of crispy shallots. Serve alongside the roasted vine tomatoes, topped with a sprinkling of parsley.

VEGAN
PREP TIME: 20 MINUTES
+ 2 HOURS CHILLING
NO COOKING TIME
SERVES 6

WATERMELON & MINT GAZPACHO

5 medium tomatoes, deseeded
¼ small watermelon
    (approx. 300g), skin removed
    and cut into chunks
1 garlic clove, crushed
2 tbsp red white vinegar
Small handful of mint, leaves
    picked
2 tbsp extra virgin olive oil,
    plus extra for drizzling
150ml tomato juice
Salt and freshly ground
    black pepper

I first tasted this in Mauritius while on holiday. I've tried several versions since then, and I have to tell you there is no fresher lunch than this. Even friends who don't like gazpacho like this, and it works great if you knock up a batch for a BBQ and serve it chilled. Check you out, chef!

1 In a food processor, blitz the tomatoes, watermelon, garlic, vinegar, mint and olive oil until you have a smooth, thick base.

2 Add in the tomato juice and blitz again. Season well with salt and pepper and taste the soup to make sure you are happy with it.

3 Pour the gazpacho into a container and refrigerate for at least 2 hours until the soup is really cold, then serve drizzled with olive oil.

VEGAN
PREP TIME: 10 MINUTES
COOKING TIME: 30 MINUTES
SERVES 2

ITALIAN TOMATO BARLEY RISOTTO

3 tbsp olive oil
1 red onion, finely chopped
2 garlic cloves, crushed
200g sundried tomatoes
300g pearl barley
150ml white wine
1 litre vegetable stock
2 tbsp finely chopped parsley
2 tbsp finely chopped basil
150g cherry vine tomatoes
Salt and freshly ground
    black pepper

Ok, now I've put a risotto in because people like to know how to make risotto, but can I just say to all restaurant owners, the last thing a veggie or vegan diner wants to hear when they ask what's on the menu for them is, 'we have a lovely risotto'. Bear in mind that there are 100 recipes in this book alone and all you ever get offered is a risotto. So here's my risotto.

1 Heat 2 tablespoons of the olive oil in a large non-stick saucepan over a medium–low heat. Add the onion along with a good pinch of salt and gently fry for 10 minutes or until softened. Add the garlic and sundried tomatoes and cook for a further minute. Add the barley, pour in the white wine, then bring to the boil and reduce the liquid by half. Tip in a quarter of the stock and cook, stirring continuously, until the barley has absorbed most of the stock, then continue adding ladles of the liquid, still continuing to stir, until you are left with a loose dropping consistency – this should take 20–25 minutes. Stir through the parsley and basil and season to taste.

2 In a small frying pan, add the remaining oil and gently fry the vine tomatoes for 2–3 minutes or until turning brown.

3 Spoon generous ladles of the barley into individual serving bowls and top each with a cluster of the cherry tomatoes.

VEGAN
PREP TIME: 1 HOUR 15 MINUTES
+ 1 HOUR CHILLING
COOKING TIME: 40 MINUTES
SERVES 4

FALAFEL & ROASTED RED PEPPER NAANWICH WITH CREAMY HUMMUS

200g or ½ tin chickpeas
1 tbsp rapeseed oil
1 large shallot, finely chopped
1 tsp ground coriander
1 tsp ground cumin
2 large garlic cloves, crushed
1 large green chilli,
   finely chopped
½ large bunch of coriander,
   roughly chopped
1 tbsp plain flour
2 tbsp sesame seeds
2 red peppers
Sunflower oil, for frying
4 large plain naan breads
   or flatbreads
Salt and freshly ground
   black pepper
½ large cucumber, halved
   lengthways and sliced,
   to serve
½ large bunch of coriander,
   torn, to serve

CREAMY HUMMUS
400g tin chickpeas,
   drained and rinsed
3 tbsp tahini paste
2 small garlic cloves, crushed
Zest and juice of 1 small lemon
Salt and freshly ground
   black pepper

See what we did there? We made a sandwich into naanwich – oh, we've spent literally minutes coming up with this stuff! I actually like a naan, a stuffed naan is even better and this is lovely with some spicy tomato relish or garlic mayonnaise.

1 Drain the chickpeas and tip into the large bowl of a food processor. In a medium frying pan over a medium heat, heat the oil. Add the shallot along with a good pinch of salt, fry for 5–7 minutes or until beginning to soften and turning a light golden brown. Add the ground coriander, cumin, garlic and chilli to the pan, cooking for a further 3 minutes. Tip the shallot and spice mixture into a food processor along with the chickpeas and fresh coriander and blitz until you have a rough-textured mixture.

2 Tip into a large bowl, stir through the flour and season well to taste. Form the mixture into 14–16 patties and flatten each one gently with the palm of a damp hand. Roll briefly in sesame seeds, place on a tray and leave in the fridge for 1 hour to firm up.

3 Slice the red peppers in half, remove the stalks and scoop out the seeds using a spoon. Set on a baking tray lined with foil, skin side up. Pop under a grill heated to High and cook for 10–15 minutes or until the skin is blackened and blistered. Set aside. When cool enough to handle, gently peel off the blackened skins. Slice the flesh into chunky strips and save for later.

4 Rinse out your food processor bowl and tip in the chickpeas along with the tahini, garlic and lemon zest and juice. Blitz until combined, add 4–5 tablespoons water and blitz again for 5 minutes or until smooth and creamy. Season well to taste.

5 Heat 5cm of oil in a deep pan to 180°C, then shallow-fry the falafel in batches, until golden, and drain on kitchen paper.

6 Assemble the naanwich. Lightly grill each naan under a moderately heated grill for 2 minutes on each side or until softened and warmed through. Top half of each naan with 4 crispy falafels, a thick dollop of hummus, the roasted red pepper slices, some sliced cucumber and a handful of aromatic coriander. Fold the naan in half over the filling to create a chunky sandwich.

BORLOTTI BEAN MINESTRONE SOUP WITH BASIL & COURGETTE

4 tbsp extra virgin olive oil,
    plus extra for drizzling
2 medium onions, diced into
    ½cm pieces
2 carrots, peeled and diced
    into ½cm pieces
2 celery sticks, diced into
    ½cm pieces
1 small head of fennel, diced
3 garlic cloves, crushed
½ tsp crushed red chilli flakes
200ml white wine
400g tin chopped tomatoes
2 tbsp tomato purée
1.2–1.4 litres hot vegetable
    stock
2 bay leaves
125g small pasta shapes,
    such as conchigliette
400g tin borlotti beans,
    drained and rinsed

TO FINISH
3 small courgettes,
    sliced on the diagonal
Zest of 1 lemon
Small bunch of basil, leaves
    picked and torn
Grated Parmesan cheese
Salt and freshly ground
    black pepper

Looks good, tastes good, lovely with some torn-up chunky bread. For the pasta you can also break spaghetti into little bits and drop it in the mix, although if you can find orzo pasta that's perfect for this kind of thing and for stews.

1 Heat 3 tablespoons of olive oil in a large, heavy saucepan and cook the onions, carrots, celery and fennel over a low heat, for 15–20 minutes, until the vegetables are soft and translucent. Stir regularly to prevent the vegetables catching on the base of the pan.

2 Add in the garlic and chilli flakes before pouring in the white wine and cooking to reduce by half. Tip in the tomatoes, purée and stock, followed by the bay leaves and bring to the boil. Turn the heat down to a simmer and cook for 20 minutes with the lid off, stirring frequently.

3 Stir the pasta and borlotti beans into the soup, cooking for a further 8–10 minutes, until the pasta is tender. Turn off the heat and allow the soup to sit for a few minutes. Stir through a little more stock, if desired, to achieve a loose consistency.

4 Heat the remaining 1 tablespoon of olive oil in a small frying pan over a high heat, and, once hot, add the courgettes. Fry the courgettes for 2–3 minutes until golden, turning halfway through. Season and set aside as a garnish.

5 Finish the hot pot with the lemon zest, salt and pepper and serve in large bowls topped with a serving of courgettes, torn basil and gratings of Parmesan cheese.

VEGETARIAN
PREP TIME: 50 MINUTES
+ 1 HOUR 35 MINUTES RISING
COOKING TIME: 30 MINUTES
SERVES 6

ROASTED VEG & TALEGGIO STROMBOLI

440g strong plain flour
1½ tsp salt
7g sachet easy bake yeast
50g polenta or semolina
2 tbsp olive oil, plus extra
    for drizzling
320ml warm water

FOR THE FILLING
290g jar roasted red peppers,
    drained
280g jar sundried tomatoes,
    drained but reserving
    1–2 tbsp oil
Zest of 1 lemon
200g baby spinach
130g chargrilled artichokes,
    drained and sliced
2 tbsp capers
200g Taleggio cheese,
    roughly chopped
½ small bunch of basil, chopped
Salt and freshly ground
    black pepper

So a pizza is flat, a calzone is folded over and a Stromboli is a pizza turned into a large sausage roll so that the filling doesn't slide off. A pizza that is a sausage roll, what's not to like?

1 First make the dough. Sift the flour and salt into a large bowl, adding the yeast and 40g of the polenta or semolina. Combine well, making a dip in the middle of the dry ingredients. Add the olive oil and warm water. Mix the dough together using a wooden spoon at first and then your hands. Turn out onto a lightly floured surface and knead for 5 minutes until smooth and springy. Set aside to a warm place in a large, lightly oiled bowl covered with a damp tea towel. Allow to rise for about 1 hour or until doubled in size.

2 To make the filling, tip half the peppers and half the sundried tomatoes into the small bowl of a food processor and blitz with the reserved 1–2 tablespoons of oil and the lemon zest until you have a smooth paste. Season to taste and set aside in a small bowl. Slice the remaining peppers into strips and roughly chop the remaining tomatoes.

3 Add the spinach to a saucepan with ½ tablespoon of water, cover and cook for 5 minutes over a low heat or until wilted. Place the spinach in a sieve and use the back of a large spoon to squeeze out as much of the excess liquid as possible.

Recipe continued overleaf

Recipe continued

4 Preheat the oven to 200°C/fan 180°C/gas 6. Once the dough has doubled in size, tip it out onto a lightly floured surface and use your fists to knock out as much air as possible. Roll out the dough to a rectangle measuring 44 x 30cm. Spread the pepper and tomato paste evenly over the rolled-out dough, scatter over the chopped peppers, tomatoes, spinach, artichokes and capers. Top with the Taleggio and basil and season well with a little more black pepper. Tuck the two shorter ends of the stromboli in and, starting from the top, firmly roll it up, working towards you. Place the stromboli, seal side down, on a lined baking sheet and leave to rise for 35 minutes, covered with lightly oiled cling film. Sprinkle with the remaining polenta and an extra drizzle of olive oil and bake for 30 minutes or until golden brown. Slice into warm chunky slices while the cheese is still gooey or simply leave to cool down and enjoy at a picnic or for lunch.

GNOCCHI WITH POMODORO SAUCE

FOR THE GNOCCHI
700g floury potatoes
250g pasta or strong
   plain flour
4 large sage leaves,
   finely chopped
Salt and freshly ground
   black pepper

FOR THE SAUCE
2 tbsp olive oil
1 medium onion, chopped
2 fat garlic cloves, crushed
½ tsp dried chilli flakes
2 x 400g tins chopped tomatoes
½ tbsp red wine vinegar
½ tbsp soft brown sugar
50ml milk
½ small bunch of basil, chopped,
   plus extra to serve
40g Parmesan cheese, shaved
Salt and freshly ground
   black pepper

Gnocchi is Italian for stay home under a duvet and eat comfort food. It's not actually, but it should be. Great dish.

1 First make the gnocchi. Bring a large pan of salted water to the boil. Add the potatoes, whole and still in their skins, and boil for 15–20 minutes or until tender when a cutlery knife is inserted into them. Drain and leave to cool for 10 minutes. Once cooled, peel off the skins and pass the flesh through a potato ricer or mash it with a fork – try not to overwork it. Place the potato, flour, sage and seasoning in a bowl and gently mix together. You may not need to use all the flour, so add it in gradually or until the mixture isn't sticking to your fingers. Divide the mixture into 5 chunks. Roll each piece into a long 2cm-thick sausage. Cut the sausage into 3cm nuggets. Repeat with the remaining pieces. Place on a baking tray and set aside in the fridge.

2 In a large casserole pot or saucepan, heat the olive oil. Add the onion and cook on a medium heat for 10 minutes or until softened and translucent. Add the garlic and chilli and cook for 1 minute. Stir in the tomatoes as well as the red wine vinegar and sugar. Bring the liquid to the boil, reduce to a simmer, cover and cook gently over a low–medium heat for 35–45 minutes or until the sauce has reduced by a third and become thicker in texture. Stir through the milk and basil and season to taste.

3 Bring a large pan of salted water to the boil. Add the gnocchi and cook for 3–4 minutes or until they begin to bob gently to the surface. Drain and toss with the tomato sauce. Spoon into bowls and top with large shavings of the cheese and a few basil leaves.

WHITE BEAN PURÉE WITH BLACK OLIVES & GOAT'S CHEESE

1 tbsp olive oil
1 small onion, finely diced
2 x 400g tins butter beans, drained and rinsed
6 thyme sprigs, leaves stripped and finely chopped
1 rosemary sprig, leaves stripped and finely chopped
2 tbsp crème fraîche
60g black pitted olives, roughly chopped
60g soft goat's cheese
Salt and freshly ground black pepper

It's the thyme and rosemary that make this, I think, so try to use fresh herbs rather than dried, if you can.

1 Heat the olive oil in a medium saucepan and sauté the onion with 1 tablespoon of water over a low heat for 10 minutes. Once soft, tip the butter beans into the pan along with the thyme, rosemary and some salt and pepper. Cook over a medium heat for 3 minutes until fragrant and the beans have softened slightly.

2 While the mixture is still hot, pour it into a food processor along with 2 tablespoons hot water, or use a stick blender in the pan, and blitz until you have a smooth purée.

3 Return the mix to the pan or a large serving bowl and stir through the crème fraîche with the olives, then crumble in the goat's cheese – try to keep it in nice large chunks. Season well and serve straight away.

CORONATION CHICKPEAS

2 tbsp raisins
2 tsp olive oil
400g tin chickpeas,
    rinsed and drained
½ tbsp mild curry powder
¼ tbsp ground cumin
75ml soya milk
1 tbsp tahini paste
¼ tsp salt

On my return from Thailand, while trying hard to keep going with my veggie-vegan lifestyle, I came across O' Joy restaurant in Shrewsbury, which serves really good vegan food. I met the owner, who invited me to become a co-owner. It seemed like a good idea at the time, so I've been in the vegan restaurant business for over a year now. It's never going to make me a fortune, but it is introducing more and more people to vegan food with a friendly, non-judgemental vibe. This is an easy recipe from Carlos and Becky that we use all the time and which customers love.

1 Put the raisins in a bowl and pour hot water over them. Allow to plump up for 20 minutes, then drain and set aside.

2 Heat the olive oil in a large frying pan and add the chickpeas, curry powder and cumin. Heat through over a high heat for 2–3 minutes then pour in the soya milk. Transfer the chickpeas to a food processor and blitz with the tahini and salt. If needed, add a little more olive oil to achieve a soft dropping consistency.

3 Roughly chop up the raisins and stir into the mix, taste and add more salt, if needed. Decant into a bowl and serve as a dip or a sandwich filler.

WASABI VIRGIN MARY SOUP

2 tbsp olive oil
1 red onion, finely chopped
2 celery sticks, finely chopped
1 small garlic clove, crushed
½ small red chilli, deseeded
   and chopped
2 large jarred roasted
   peppers, sliced
2 x 400g tins plum tomatoes
200g cherry tomatoes
400ml vegetable stock
2 tbsp brown sugar
2 tbsp lemon juice
60g stale bread
2 tbsp Worcestershire sauce
1 tsp Tabasco
½ small bunch of flat-leaf
   parsley, finely chopped
100ml buttermilk
100g crème fraîche
3 tbsp milk
1 tsp wasabi paste
A handful of pea shoots
   (optional)
Salt and freshly ground
   black pepper

To be fair, this recipe does what it says on the tin, except it's not in a tin, it's wrestled onto the table to impress people from your own fair or calloused hands.

1 Heat the olive oil in a large casserole dish or saucepan over a low heat. Add the onion and celery and cook gently with a pinch of salt for 10 minutes or until the onion is soft and translucent. Add the garlic and chilli and cook for 2 minutes. Add the peppers, both sets of tomatoes and the stock and bring to the boil. Reduce to a simmer, stir through the brown sugar, lemon juice and stale bread and cook gently, covered, for 20 minutes.

2 Tip the soup into a blender or use a stick blender in the pan to blitz it to a smooth texture. Stir the Worcestershire sauce, Tabasco and parsley through the soup and season to taste. Set aside over a low heat to warm through.

3 In a small bowl, mix together the buttermilk, crème fraîche, milk and wasabi. Season with salt. Ladle the soup into individual serving bowls and drizzle over the wasabi crème fraîche. Top each with a cluster of the curly peppery pea shoots, if using, then serve.

SESAME NOODLE SALAD WITH SOY

200g flat rice noodles
1 tbsp sesame oil
200g smoked tofu or
    marinated tofu, chopped
1 medium red chilli,
    deseeded and thinly sliced
5 spring onions, sliced
100g beansprouts
5 radishes, sliced
½ small bunch of mint, chopped
½ bunch of basil, chopped
3 tbsp sesame seeds
3 tbsp cashew nuts, chopped
Salt

FOR THE DRESSING
4 tbsp sesame oil
2 tbsp rice wine vinegar
Juice of ½ lime
2 tbsp dark soy sauce

Lovely and fresh, and slightly salty. I don't eat a lot of tofu but this is one recipe that it's worth trying it in.

1 Bring a large pan of lightly salted water to the boil and add the noodles. Cook for 10–15 minutes or until just cooked. Drain and leave to rest in a bowl of ice-cold water.

2 In a small pan, heat 1 tablespoon of the sesame oil, then add the tofu and fry gently over a medium heat for 5 minutes or until golden brown.

3 Meanwhile, make the dressing. Whisk together the sesame oil, vinegar, lime juice and soy sauce.

4 Drain the noodles, tip them into a large bowl and toss together with the dressing. Mix through the tofu, chilli, spring onions, beansprouts, radishes, half the mint and half the basil. Top with the sesame seeds, cashew nuts and remaining herbs. Bundle into deep bowls and enjoy.

THAI GREEN CURRY TOM YUM

3 tbsp sunflower oil
2 shallots, finely chopped
1 green pepper, deseeded
   and thinly sliced
100g chestnut mushrooms,
   sliced
1 garlic clove, crushed
3 tbsp Thai green curry paste
400g tin full-fat coconut milk
450ml hot vegetable stock
1 lemongrass stick,
   lightly bashed
1 star anise
150g pack of vermicelli
   rice noodles
100g frozen soya beans

TO SERVE
Juice of 1 lime
Handful of coriander or Thai
   basil, roughly chopped
1 green bird's-eye chilli,
   thinly sliced
Salt and freshly ground
   black pepper

The fresh, zingy, aromatic flavours in a Thai curry dish are so so good, and infused into curry milk you could eat the sole of your work boot in it and it would taste good. Luckily this has got veg instead.

1 Heat the oil in a large saucepan over a medium heat. Add the shallots and pepper and fry gently for 8–10 minutes or until everything begins to soften. Add the mushroom slices and fry for a further 3 minutes. Finally, add the garlic and curry paste and cook for 1 minute.

2 Shake the tin of coconut milk to ensure it is mixed well, then open it and pour it into the pan with the vegetable stock. Bring to the boil then reduce to a simmer, add the whole lemongrass and star anise and allow the soup to simmer gently for 15 minutes.

3 Once the broth is aromatic, steep the rice noodles in a bowl of boiling water for 3 minutes, then drain. Cook the soya beans in a pan of boiling water for 3 minutes, then drain and refresh under running water.

4 Divide the noodles and beans among 4 deep bowls and ladle over the soup. Add a squeeze of lime juice to each portion, then top with the coriander and slices of bird's-eye chilli, depending on your heat preference, and season to taste.

HANGOVER NOODLES

FOR THE SAUCE
4 tbsp dark soy sauce
2 tbsp runny honey
3 tbsp sriracha hot sauce
    (depending on how hot you
    like it!), plus extra to serve
1 tbsp oyster sauce
1 tsp toasted sesame oil
Few drops of Worcestershire
    sauce
Freshly ground black pepper

FOR THE STIR-FRY
2 tbsp vegetable oil
265g pack of stir-fry mix
    vegetables
300g straight-to-wok rice
    noodles
4 medium eggs
Small handful of cashew
    nuts, roughly chopped
Small handful of coriander
    leaves, roughly chopped
1 lime, cut into wedges

Ok, the recipe below needs very little explanation. When you're having one of those 'recovery days' and need something to clear your mouth that's like the bottom of a parrot's cage, settle the stomach and make you feel human again without too much effort, this should be your comfort food of choice.

1 In a small bowl, stir together all the ingredients for the sauce and put to one side.

2 Heat half of the oil in a large frying pan or wok until it is really hot, then throw in the stir-fry veg.

3 Throw the noodles into the pan and mix everything together well – and quickly! – then pour the sauce over and stir to combine. Turn off the heat and put to one side while you fry the eggs.

4 Heat the remaining oil in a shallow frying pan and crack in the eggs, cooking them for 1–2 minutes on a high heat until the edges are crispy but the yolks are still runny.

5 Finish the noodles with a handful of cashews, the coriander leaves and a squeeze of lime before topping each plate with an egg and a little extra sriracha sauce.

VEGETARIAN
PREP TIME: 10 MINUTES
COOKING TIME: 25 MINUTES
SERVES 4

FILLLING CAULIFLOWER & SWEETCORN CHOWDER

1 tbsp olive oil
1 onion, finely chopped
½ cauliflower head (approx. 300g), cut into small florets
1 celery stick, finely chopped
3 garlic cloves, crushed
1 red chilli, deseeded and finely chopped
1 tsp smoked paprika
1 floury potato (approx. 250g), peeled and cut into small dice
1 tbsp plain flour
500ml semi-skimmed milk
200g tin sweetcorn, drained
A handful of flat leaf parsley, leaves picked and chopped
A handful of chives, finely chopped
Salt and freshly ground black pepper
Warm bread, to serve

Cauliflower farmers must have wondered if it was worth carrying on or if they should switch to wheat grass a few years back, but now they're in the money as veggies and vegans are mad for this vegetable. It's chunky, takes on other flavours well and goes nutty when roasted until brown. So here's a thick soup or chowder made with it. Even if you're not a fan of cauliflower, try this – it is so full of flavours, you'll love it.

1 Heat the oil in a large, heavy-based pan over a medium heat. Add the onion, cauliflower, celery, garlic, chilli and paprika and cook gently for 4–5 minutes until the onion has become translucent. Stir through the potato and flour and cook for a minute or so.

2 Pour over the milk – it should just cover the potatoes – and continue to cook over a medium heat for 14–16 minutes, or until the potatoes and cauliflower are tender. Stir through the corn and allow to heat through. Purée half the soup using a stick blender or gently mash with a potato masher. Return the blended soup to the pan and add enough milk to achieve your desired soup consistency. Reheat gently, seasoning to taste.

3 Serve sprinkled with parsley and chives and with chunks of fresh bread alongside.

VEGAN
PREP TIME: 10 MINUTES
+ 15 MINUTES MARINATING
COOKING TIME: 10 MINUTES
SERVES 2

TOFU PAD THAI

2 tbsp light soy sauce
1 tbsp tamarind paste
1 tsp runny honey
1 garlic clove, finely grated
2cm piece of ginger,
  peeled and finely grated
200g firm tofu, cut into
  2cm chunks
100g dried rice ribbon noodles
1 tbsp vegetable oil
80g beansprouts
50g salted peanuts,
  roughly chopped
Small handful of coriander
  leaves, roughly chopped
1 small cucumber, cut into
  sticks, to serve
1 lime, cut into wedges,
  to serve

Everyone likes pad Thai, but not everyone likes tofu, so if you can find it there's a mushroom called 'chicken of the woods' (I kid you not, the genus is Laetiporus), which you can cut into strips and fry like steak. It's a great alternative.

1 In a small bowl, whisk together the soy sauce, tamarind, honey, garlic and ginger. Add the tofu to the mixture and leave to marinate for 15 minutes.

2 Put the noodles in a large bowl and cover with boiling water. Leave for 5 minutes and then drain. They should be softened but not fully cooked at this point.

3 Heat the oil in a large frying pan until really hot. Carefully add the tofu and marinade, then cook on high for 2 minutes until slightly charred and dark brown. Toss in the drained noodles and cook for another 30 seconds.

4 Remove the pan from the heat and throw in the beansprouts, peanuts and coriander. Dish up and serve with the cucumber sticks and lime wedges on the side.

VEGAN
PREP TIME: 25 MINUTES
COOKING TIME: 50 MINUTES
SERVES 4

SPICY RAMEN WITH TOFU & SESAME

4 tbsp sesame oil
6 spring onions, sliced
1 thumb-sized piece of ginger, peeled and grated
2 fat garlic cloves, crushed
1 red chilli, deseeded and finely chopped
3 tbsp white miso paste
1 litre veg stock
2 star anise
3 tbsp light soy sauce, plus extra to serve (optional)
160g soba noodles
100g baby spinach
1 tbsp chilli oil
200g smoked tofu, cut into thick slices
1½ tbsp sesame seeds
100g beansprouts
1 tbsp Dulse seeweed (optional)

So the Chinese and Japanese have been arguing for some time over who invented ramen. It probably originated in Mongolia. Either way, I've been in noodle houses in Japan where it's good manners to suck your noodles up spaghetti-style, making as much noise as possible. Tell the family this and have a noisy, fun and tasty meal.

1 Heat 3 tablespoons of the sesame oil in a deep saucepan over a medium heat. Add half the spring onions, the ginger, garlic and half the chilli. Fry gently for 5–7 minutes before stirring through the miso paste. Stir to combine and pour in the stock and star anise. Bring to the boil, reduce to a simmer and cook, uncovered, for 20–25 minutes until all the flavours have combined well. Stir through the soy sauce.

2 Meanwhile, bring a large pan of salted water to the boil. Add the noodles and gently boil for 4–5 minutes, before quickly straining and running under cold water to stop the cooking process. Drizzle with the remaining sesame oil and set aside. Place the spinach in a small pan over a medium heat along with 1 teaspoon of water, then cover and cook for 3 minutes or until wilted.

3 Heat the chilli oil in a frying pan over a medium heat. Add the tofu slices and fry on either side for 3 minutes or until golden brown and lightly crisp. Set aside on kitchen paper and sprinkle with the sesame seeds.

4 Ladle the broth into 2 deep bowls, fill with a generous nest of noodles and a handful of beansprouts, then top with the remaining chilli, tofu, spinach and remaining spring onion. Sprinkle over the seaweed, if you wish, if not, pour over an extra glug of salty soy sauce.

VEGAN
PREP TIME: 35 MINUTES
+ 1 HOUR CHILLING
COOKING TIME: 15 MINUTES
SERVES 2

NOODLE BOWL WITH ASIAN PICKLED VEG

FOR THE PICKLES
1 medium carrot
3 radishes
¼ cucumber
200ml rice wine vinegar
50g caster sugar
½ tsp salt
10cm piece ginger,
   peeled and grated
1 tbsp nigella seeds

FOR THE NOODLES
5 tbsp sesame oil
1 medium red chilli, deseeded
   and finely chopped
4 tbsp crunchy peanut butter
200g soba noodles
40g unsalted peanuts,
   roughly chopped
¼ small bunch of Thai basil
   or coriander
2 tbsp mint leaves, chopped
Sriracha hot sauce or sweet
   chilli sauce, to serve
   (optional)

So this one is a bit more complicated, but not a lot really. Making the pickles is easy and I really love pickles – not just piccalilli and gherkins, but pickled walnuts and figs too. This is a mild pickle but it makes this such a different and unusual dish. Give it a go.

1 Make the pickles. Using a peeler, cut thin ribbons off the carrot and set aside, finely slice the radishes and cut them in half, then thinly slice the cucumber. In a small saucepan over a low heat, heat the vinegar, sugar, salt, ginger and 100ml water gently for 5 minutes or until the sugar has completely dissolved, then stir through the nigella seeds. Pop the carrot slices, radishes and cucumber into a Kilner jar or bowl. Pour the pickling liquid over the veg and leave for a minimum of 1 hour in the fridge.

2 Pour the sesame oil into a small frying pan and add the chilli. Heat the oil over a medium heat and cook the chilli for 3 minutes or until it begins to pop and sizzle. Remove from the heat and tip into a bowl. Whisk in the peanut butter and set aside.

3 Bring a large pan of water to the boil. Add the noodles and blanch for 3 minutes – be careful not to overcook them, they can quickly turn soft and stodgy. Drain and toss with the peanut dressing while the noodles are still hot. Set aside to cool to room temperature.

4 Heat a small pan over a medium heat, add the peanuts and toast for 2–3 minutes or until a nice even brown. Bundle the noodles into 2 deep bowls, top with a small handful of the drained pickles, the chopped and toasted nuts and the Asian basil or coriander and the mint. Finish by spooning over 2–3 tablespoons of the pickling liquid and a good drizzle of sriracha or chilli sauce, if you like.

THREE
THE MAIN
EVENT

VEGGIE BEAN TACOS & CORIANDER YOGHURT

1 tbsp olive oil
1 medium onion, finely chopped
1 green pepper, deseeded
  and finely sliced
1 red pepper, deseeded
  and finely sliced
1 garlic clove, crushed
½ red chilli, deseeded and
  finely chopped
2 tbsp smoked paprika
½ tsp hot cayenne pepper
2 tbsp soft dark brown sugar
400g tin chopped tomatoes,
  drained
2 x 400g tins black beans,
  rinsed and drained
Juice of 1 lime
Salt and freshly ground
  black pepper

**FOR THE CORIANDER
YOGHURT**
150g coconut milk yoghurt
  or natural yoghurt
Zest and juice of 1 lime
Small bunch of coriander,
  leaves finely chopped
½ tsp salt

TO SERVE
8 taco shells, warmed according
  to the packet instructions
1 large green chilli, deseeded
  and finely sliced
1 small red onion, finely sliced
½ small bunch of coriander, torn

This is just lovely. I'm aware that some people don't like coriander, so for those that don't, parsley will stand in nicely. A little avocado wouldn't hurt on this, too. For extra richness add a cube or two of dark chocolate to the bean mix.

1 Heat the olive oil in a large casserole dish or saucepan over a medium heat. Add the onion and cook for 8–10 minutes or until beginning to soften and brown slightly. Add the peppers and cook for a further 5 minutes. Add the garlic and chilli along with the paprika and cayenne and cook for 2 minutes. Then stir through the brown sugar and tomatoes. Add the drained beans, bring to the boil, reduce to a very gentle simmer and cook for 25 minutes, uncovered, until thickened. Season to taste with the lime juice, salt and pepper.

2 Make the coriander yoghurt by gently combining the yoghurt, lime zest and juice, coriander and salt in a bowl.

3 Generously spoon the bean chilli into the crunchy taco shells. Top with the green chilli, red onion, coriander and a dollop of the coriander yoghurt.

VEGAN
PREP TIME: 20 MINUTES
COOKING TIME: 40 MINUTES
SERVES 4

WILD MUSHROOM & SPINACH RISOTTO

30g dried wild mushrooms
4 tbsp extra virgin olive oil,
 plus extra for drizzling
1 medium onion, finely diced
1 garlic clove, crushed
280g Arborio risotto rice
130ml white wine
800ml hot vegetable stock
3 portobello mushrooms
¼ tsp dried thyme
100g spinach leaves
Salt and freshly ground
 black pepper

It's a risotto. It's got mushrooms and spinach and it's easy once you've done it for the first time. You'll be making your own in no time.

1 Put the dried mushrooms into a jug and cover with 400ml boiling water. Put to one side. Heat half the olive oil in a wide frying pan and throw in the onion and garlic. Add 2 tablespoons of water to the pan and cook over a low heat for 8–10 minutes, until soft.

2 Tip in the rice and stir well, making sure it is covered in the onion and oil mix. Then add the white wine and stir until it has all been absorbed by the rice. Next, add in the stock, a large glug at a time, stirring constantly, waiting until the rice has absorbed the majority of the stock before pouring in the next bit. This can take up to 20–25 minutes from start to finish, so don't worry if it's taking a while.

3 Drain the dried mushrooms and roughly chop them, then throw them into the risotto pan.

4 In a separate frying pan, heat the remaining 2 tablespoons of olive oil over a high heat. Brush the portobello mushrooms with a dry tea towel to remove any dirt and then slice into 1.5cm-wide steaks. Fry the mushrooms for about 5 minutes until golden, toss over the thyme and put to one side.

5 Taste the risotto to check the rice is tender but with a little bite to it and season with salt and pepper to taste. Stir the spinach leaves through the hot risotto until they are wilted – about 30 seconds – and then plate up a large spoonful topped with the mushroom steaks and drizzled with a little more extra virgin olive oil.

RATATOUILLE CASSEROLE WITH FETA

3 tbsp olive oil
2 large red onions, quartered
2 courgettes, chopped
1 large aubergine, chopped
1 red pepper, deseeded
  and finely sliced
2 garlic cloves, crushed
2 tbsp chopped thyme leaves
½ tsp chilli flakes
2 x 400g tins chopped tomatoes
200g cherry tomatoes
60g pitted black olives
80g pearl barley
200ml vegetable stock
1 tbsp red wine vinegar
1 tbsp soft brown sugar
3 wholemeal pittas, cut into
  bite-sized pieces
1 tsp dried mixed herbs
200g feta cheese, crumbled
Salt and freshly ground
  black pepper

I think you either like ratatouille or you don't. My mate took his West Country-farmer dad to a posh restaurant where, after gazing at the menu for ages, he announced to the waiter, 'I'll have some o' that there rat tat willie'. He liked it, too, by all accounts.

1 Preheat the oven to 180°C/fan 160°C/gas 4.

2 Heat 2 tablespoons of the oil in a large casserole pot over a medium heat. Add the red onions, courgettes, aubergine and pepper to the pan and cook, covered, for 8–10 minutes or until everything is softened. Add the garlic, 1 tablespoon of the thyme and the chilli and cook for a further 2 minutes. Stir through the chopped tomatoes, whole cherry tomatoes, olives, barley and stock, along with the vinegar and sugar. Bring the pan to the boil, reduce to a simmer and cook, covered, for 20 minutes or until everything is slightly thickened and reduced. Season to taste.

3 Toss the pitta pieces with the remaining oil and the dried herbs and spread out on a baking sheet. Place in the oven for 8–10 minutes, turning halfway through cooking.

4 Remove the lid from the casserole and top the ratatouille with the pitta and crumbled feta, as well as the remaining thyme and a good grind of black pepper. Return to the oven and bake, uncovered, for 15–20 minutes or until the pitta is golden brown and the ratatouille is bubbling. Serve in deep bowls.

VEGAN
PREP TIME: 30 MINUTES
COOKING TIME: 45 MINUTES
SERVES 4

VEGETABLE KOFTAS IN SPICY COCONUT & TOMATO SAUCE

FOR THE KOFTAS

½ small head of cauliflower, florets chopped into 1cm pieces
2.5 litres vegetable oil
2 carrots, peeled and grated
1 small onion, sliced into half moons
Small bunch of coriander, leaves and stalks finely chopped
135g gram flour
1 tsp ground turmeric
2 tsp garam masala
¼ tsp chilli powder
200g unsweetened coconut yoghurt
Salt and freshly ground black pepper

FOR THE SAUCE

1 small onion, quartered
1 garlic clove
1 red chilli, seeds in
2cm piece of ginger, peeled and roughly chopped
2 tbsp coconut oil
6 green cardamom pods, bashed
1 tbsp yellow mustard seeds
260g cherry tomatoes, cut in half
400g tin coconut milk
1 tbsp tomato purée

Coriander leaves and warm naan bread, to serve

If you're wondering what a kofta is, it's a strangely shaped meatball, only we're not doing meat so this is a chunky veg version in a sauce that will light up your taste buds.

1 Preheat the oven to 190°C/fan 170°C/gas 5.

2 Spread the cauliflower florets on a large baking tray and drizzle with 1 tablespoon of the vegetable oil and season with salt and pepper. Roast in the oven for 20 minutes until just tender and slightly charred. Set aside to cool slightly. Turn the oven down to 150°C/fan 130°C/gas 2.

3 In a large mixing bowl, combine the carrots, onion, roasted cauliflower and coriander. Once mixed, add in the gram flour, spices and yoghurt along with salt and pepper and stir together well. You should be left with a thick, golden batter.

4 Pour the remaining oil into a large saucepan and heat. Check it is hot by dropping ½ teaspoon of the batter into the oil. It should sizzle and float to the surface, turning golden after 15 seconds. Use 2 spoons or an ice-cream scoop to portion the batter into 16 koftas and fry in batches of 3–4, cooking each for 15–20 seconds until golden. Drain the koftas, once fried, on kitchen paper and place in the low oven to keep warm while you make the sauce.

Recipe continued overleaf

Recipe continued

5 Place the onion, garlic, chilli and ginger in a food processor with a splash of water and blitz until you have a coarse paste. Heat the coconut oil in a saucepan and fry the cardamom and mustard seeds until they start to pop.

6 Add the onion mixture to the pan and fry, over a medium heat, for 5–7 minutes until it starts to turn slightly golden. Carefully add in the tomatoes, frying for 1 minute and finish with the coconut milk and tomato purée. Bring the sauce to the boil, then turn down to a simmer, uncovered, for 7–10 minutes, until it has thickened slightly and the tomatoes have broken down a little. Season with salt to taste.

7 To serve, place the koftas in pasta bowls and spoon over the sauce or serve the sauce alongside. Garnish with fresh coriander and serve with warm naan breads.

VEGETARIAN
PREP TIME: 20 MINUTES
+ OVERNIGHT SOAKING
COOKING TIME: 2 HOURS 20 MINUTES
SERVES 4

BLACK BEAN CHILLI WITH SMOKED CHIPOTLE & RED PEPPER

250g dried black beans
1 chipotle chilli or
  ½ tsp chilli flakes
2 tbsp olive oil
2 onions, sliced
3 garlic cloves, sliced
1 tsp ground cumin
1 tsp smoked paprika
350ml passata
1 tbsp tomato purée
2 red peppers, deseeded
  and sliced
1 large courgette, sliced
Salt and freshly ground
  black pepper

TO SERVE
4 tbsp sour cream
1 avocado, sliced
1 lime, cut into quarters
2 tbsp chopped coriander
  leaves

Chilli is always good – we all know what a good feed chilli can be. You can add some veggie mince to make it bigger but it's the smoked chipotle that gives this its outstanding taste.

1 Put the dried beans into a large bowl, cover with cold water and leave to soak overnight.

2 Drain the beans and rinse thoroughly. Cover with 1–1.5 litres of cold water and bring to the boil. Allow the beans to simmer for 50 minutes–1 hour until the beans are just tender, skimming off and discarding any foam that rises to the surface.

3 Meanwhile, prepare the sauce. Pour 500ml boiling water over a whole dried chipotle chilli and allow to soak for 5 minutes. Remove the chilli from the water (keeping the liquid), squeeze out any excess water and finely slice the chilli.

4 Heat the olive oil in a large casserole pot over a medium–high heat. Add the onions and cook for 3–4 minutes until slightly golden and softened. Add the garlic, chopped chipotle chilli (or chilli flakes, if you are using), cumin and paprika and cook for a further 2 minutes. Add the passata and tomato purée and simmer over a gentle heat for 15 minutes.

5 Drain the black beans and add them to the pot along with the liquid from the smoked chipotle. Add the peppers and courgette and simmer for 40–50 minutes until it has all come together and is lovely and tender.

6 Serve the chilli with dollops of sour cream, avocado, lime wedges and coriander leaves.

RICH LENTIL BOLOGNESE

2 tbsp olive oil
1 large onion, finely diced
2 carrots, peeled and
    diced into ½cm pieces
2 celery sticks, diced into
    ½cm pieces
½ tbsp fresh or dried oregano,
    finely chopped
3–4 rosemary sprigs
3–4 thyme sprigs
1 garlic clove, crushed
200ml full-bodied red wine
400g tin green lentils, rinsed
    and drained
2 x 400g tins chopped tomatoes
1 tbsp tomato purée
2 tsp sugar
1 bay leaf
360g dried spaghetti (or
    other pasta of your choice)
Salt and freshly ground
    black pepper
Grated Parmesan cheese
    (if not required to be vegan),
    to serve
Basil or rocket leaves, to serve

This is man's best friend, recipe wise, only swapping the mince for lentils. That said, you do have to work to make lentils interesting, as they can be about as appetising as cardboard, but I think you'll be surprised at how good this Bolognese is.

1 Heat the olive oil in a large saucepan over a low heat and add in the onion along with a pinch of salt and splash of water, then sweat for 10 minutes until really soft. Stir through the carrots, celery and oregano. Tie the rosemary and thyme sprigs together with kitchen string and add to the pot. Continue to cook, over a low heat, for a further 15 minutes. Stir through the garlic and soften for a further minute before pouring in the red wine. Simmer until the liquid has reduced by half, 1–2 minutes. Next, tip in the lentils, chopped tomatoes, tomato purée and sugar. Season well and bring the pot to a boil. Nestle in the bay leaf and reduce to a simmer. Cook, uncovered, for 20 minutes, stirring occasionally, until the sauce has thickened slightly.

2 Meanwhile, bring a large pan of salted water to the boil and cook the pasta for 6–8 minutes until 'al dente', then drain.

3 Remove the herb bundle from the sauce and pour the Bolognese over the drained pasta and toss to coat it well. Serve with Parmesan (if using) and basil or rocket leaves scattered over.

VEGAN
PREP TIME: 40 MINUTES
+ 2 HOURS CHILLING
NO COOKING TIME
SERVES 4

RAW LASAGNE WITH VEGAN RICOTTA & SUNDRIED TOMATOES

FOR THE TOMATO PASTE
4 tbsp tomato purée
400g sundried tomatoes
4 tsp maple syrup
6 thyme sprigs, leaves picked

FOR THE WALNUT RICOTTA
200g walnut halves, soaked
    overnight in cold water
1 tbsp extra virgin olive oil
¼ whole nutmeg, grated
Salt and freshly ground
    black pepper

FOR THE PISTACHIO PESTO
100g shelled pistachios
80g basil leaves, plus extra
    for serving
95ml extra virgin olive oil
1 garlic clove

FOR THE LASAGNE
2 medium courgettes, sliced
    thinly lengthways

This recipe is fiddly and posh but it will get you a good deal of love and attention for the effort. It's a vegan's dream and everyone else I've made it for loves it – very fresh and summery. Actually, I got served this in the Maldives and asked the chef who made it to write the ingredients down. He did, but he spoke no English and couldn't explain how to do it – and he also gave no amounts or instructions. So, after much experimenting myself, here it is.

1 First make the tomato paste. In a food processor or blender, blitz together the tomato purée, sundried tomatoes, maple syrup and thyme leaves until you have a thick paste. Scrape into a bowl and set aside.

2 Rinse out the food processor bowl and drain the walnuts from their soaking water. Blend these with 100ml water and the extra virgin olive oil until you have a white, thick, ricotta-like mixture, then pour into a bowl. Taste and season with salt, pepper and nutmeg. Set aside.

3 Lastly, make the pesto by blitzing the pistachios with the basil, 2 tablespoons of the olive oil and garlic, then gradually pour in the remaining olive oil to make a thick, vibrant, green paste.

4 In a lasagne dish about 30 x 18cm, place a layer of the sliced courgette, followed by a thin layer of pesto, tomato paste and, lastly, the walnut ricotta. Repeat these layers until the dish is full, finishing with a layer of walnut ricotta topped with some freshly torn basil leaves. Put the lasagne in the fridge for at least 2 hours to set, then dig in and enjoy.

WINTER VEGGIE STEW WITH WHOLESOME LUMPY DUMPLINGS

FOR THE DUMPLINGS
50g butter, softened
125g self-raising flour
40g Cheddar cheese, crumbled
1 tbsp thyme leaves

FOR THE STEW
3 tbsp olive oil
1 large onion, roughly diced
2 celery sticks, roughly diced
3 tbsp plain flour
1 tbsp Marmite
½ tbsp tomato purée
2 litres hot vegetable stock
3 carrots, peeled and chopped
   into chunky pieces
4 parsnips, peeled and chopped
   into chunky pieces
½ head (about 450g) swede,
   peeled and chopped into
   chunky pieces
3 small sweet potatoes (500g),
   peeled and chopped into
   chunky pieces
2–3 rosemary sprigs, plus
   extra, chopped, to sprinkle
1 bouquet garni
150g orzo pasta
80g pack of cooked chestnuts,
   roughly chopped
Salt and freshly ground
   black pepper

This is one of my favourite recipes and the family get me to make this all the time. It's a big, rich, thick stew for the winter with lovely cheesy, herby dumplings, easy to make, healthy, wholesome and a proper chunky feed.

When you bung the veg into the stock, throw in a bouquet garni – you can buy these on the herb shelf in the supermarket. It's like a teabag of herbs, not very cool amongst chefs but it delivers the right amount of herby flavour without someone ending up with an inedible leaf or twig in their mouths. And chestnuts are great. We don't eat them much in this country, but they are easy to find in all big supermarkets, healthy, tasty and good for you and make the meat-free stew really hearty.

1 Start by making the dumplings. Rub the butter into the flour and mix with the Cheddar and thyme. Add just enough cold water to bring the mixture together to a soft dough and divide into 5–6 small dumplings.

2 Preheat the oven to 190°C/fan 170°C/gas 5. Heat the oil in a large casserole dish and fry the onion and celery over a low heat for 10 minutes until soft and translucent. Add the flour into the pan, whisking constantly to make a roux. Add in the Marmite and tomato purée followed by the stock, a glug at a time, whisking all the while to make a smooth base to the stew.

Recipe continued overleaf

Recipe continued

3 Throw the carrots, parsnips, swede, sweet potatoes, rosemary and bouquet garni into the dish and bring to a boil. Cook the stew, with the lid off, for 5–7 minutes. The vegetables should be cooking nicely but still have a bite to them.

4 Rinse the orzo pasta well, in a sieve, and then pour into the casserole along with the chestnuts. Season well and place the dumplings on top of the casserole. Sprinkle over a little chopped rosemary and bake in the oven, with the lid off, for 20–30 minutes until the dumplings are puffed up and nicely cooked and the vegetables are tender.

THE CLASSIC MUSHROOM STROGANOFF

30g dried mixed mushrooms
3 tbsp olive oil
1 large red onion, sliced
300g chestnut mushrooms, sliced
200g large flat mushrooms, sliced
1 tsp smoked paprika
1 large garlic clove, crushed
1 tbsp chopped thyme leaves
100ml brandy
150ml vegetable stock
150g full-fat crème fraîche
1 tbsp lemon juice
A few drops of Worcestershire sauce
½ small bunch of parsley, roughly chopped
Salt and freshly ground black pepper
Cooked tagliatelle or basmati rice, to serve

This is a great, really thick, flavoursome sauce, but you're gonna struggle if you don't like mushrooms. Even if you're not keen, though, give this try – mushrooms do taste different in a great sauce than when cooked alone, fried or watery on a builder's breakfast! If you're really unhappy about mushrooms, don't chuck this idea away; the sauce is so good, just choose a veg you really like and swap it for the 'shrooms!

1 Soak the dried mushrooms in 150ml of boiling water for 10 minutes. Heat the olive oil in a large casserole pot over a medium heat. Add the onion and cook for 5–7 minutes or until beginning to brown a little. Add the mushrooms and cook for a further 5 minutes. Stir through the paprika, garlic and thyme. Cook for 1 minute. Add the soaked mushrooms with their soaking juices as well as the brandy, bring to the boil and reduce the liquid by half. Pour in the vegetable stock and cook gently, uncovered, for 20 minutes.

2 Stir the crème fraîche through the mixture along with the lemon juice and Worcestershire sauce and cook for a further 5 minutes. Season with salt and a generous amount of black pepper. Stir through the chopped parsley and serve spooned over bowls of buttery tagliatelle or basmati rice.

MAKE IT VEGAN
Use a vegan alternative to crème fraîche.

VEGETARIAN MOUSSAKA

2 large aubergines, cut into
    cubes
2 courgettes, cut into cubes
1 large red pepper, deseeded
    and sliced
3 tbsp chopped oregano leaves
6 tbsp olive oil
2 large red onions, sliced
2 garlic cloves, crushed
3 x 400g tins chopped tomatoes
2 tbsp soft brown sugar
750ml semi-skimmed milk,
    plus 3 tbsp
1 tsp ground cinnamon
2 bay leaves
250g ready-to-eat cooked
    lentils
5 large white potatoes,
    peeled and sliced
75g unsalted butter
75g plain flour
100g strong Cheddar
    cheese, grated
2 large egg yolks
150g log goat's cheese, sliced
Salt and freshly ground
    black pepper

The trick with this is to not make the veg too wet. The layers of potato and sauce on top of this dish make it a kinda veggie hotpot with the creamiest of finishes.

1 Preheat the oven to 200°C/fan 180°C/gas 6. In a roasting tin, toss together the aubergines, the courgettes, pepper and 2 tablespoons of oregano with 2 tablespoons of olive oil and plenty of salt and pepper. Roast for 30–35 minutes or until the veg are soft.

2 Heat 2 more tablespoons of oil in a casserole dish over a medium heat. Add the red onion and cook gently for 5–10 minutes or until beginning to soften. Add the garlic and remaining oregano and cook for 2 minutes. Tip in the tomatoes, sugar, 3 tablespoons of milk, cinnamon and bay leaves. Bring to the boil, reduce to a simmer and cook for 15 minutes. Stir through the roasted veg and lentils, season and set aside.

3 Bring a large pan of salted water to the boil. Add the potatoes and boil for 6 minutes. Strain and steam dry. Spread out in a large roasting tin and toss with the remaining olive oil. Roast in the oven for 30 minutes.

4 Make the white sauce. In a large saucepan, melt the butter over a medium heat and tip in the flour, stir together and cook for 2 minutes. Take the pan off the heat and slowly whisk in the 750ml milk in several additions. Place back on the heat and cook the sauce for a further 4 minutes. Stir through the cheese and whisk through the egg yolks.

5 Assemble the moussaka. Spoon half the vegetable mix onto the base of a large ovenproof dish. Top with half the potatoes and repeat the process again. Top the dish with the white sauce and slices of goat's cheese. Bake for 40–50 minutes until golden and bubbling.

VEGETARIAN
PREP TIME: 35 MINUTES
COOKING TIME: 2 HOURS
SERVES 6

SHEPHERD'S PIE WITH A CHEESY LEEK & POTATO TOPPING

3 tbsp olive oil
1 large red onion, chopped
2 garlic cloves, crushed
2 tbsp thyme, leaves picked
1 tbsp chopped rosemary
2 large carrots, peeled
 and finely chopped
2 large parsnips, peeled and
 finely chopped
2 raw beetroots, peeled
 and cut into 2cm cubes
2 tbsp plain flour
2 tbsp tomato purée
500ml vegetable stock
1 bay leaf
250g cooked Puy lentils
3 tbsp Worcestershire sauce
Salt and freshly ground
 black pepper

FOR THE TOPPING
900g Maris Piper potatoes,
 peeled and quartered
25g salted butter
2 large leeks, trimmed and
 sliced
50ml whole milk
60g strong Cheddar cheese,
 grated
40g dried breadcrumbs
Salt and freshly ground
 black pepper

So we are back under the duvet after sticking this in the oven and filling the house with the smell of comfort food, safe in the knowledge that there's a full belly to come.

1 Heat the olive oil in a large casserole dish over a medium heat. Add the onion to the pan with a pinch of salt and cook gently until just soft. Add the garlic, 1 tablespoon of the thyme and the rosemary and cook for a further minute. Stir through the carrots, parsnips and beetroot, adding 2 tablespoons of water to the pan. Cover and cook for 8–10 minutes, until the vegetables are beginning to soften. Stir regularly, to make sure nothing is catching on the bottom of the pan.

2 Stir through the flour and tomato purée. Add a dash of the stock and bring to the boil. Pour in the remaining stock along with the bay and lentils. Cover and cook for 35–40 minutes on a low heat until the vegetables are soft. Once soft, stir through the Worcestershire sauce and season with salt and a generous amount of pepper.

3 While the base is cooking, make the topping. Bring a large pan of salted water to the boil. Add the potatoes and cook for 15 minutes or until tender. Drain and allow to steam dry for 5 minutes. Meanwhile, in a frying pan over a medium heat melt the butter, add the leeks and fry gently for 14–16 minutes until soft and collapsed. Mash the potatoes until smooth, stirring through the milk, half of the cheese and the leeks. Season to taste.

4 Preheat the oven to 180°C/fan 160°C/gas 4. Transfer the filling to a 2-litre ovenproof dish and spoon over the mash, breadcrumbs and remaining cheese and thyme. Bake for 25 minutes. Serve with steamed greens.

BRAISED SAUSAGE ALL-IN-ONE WITH CHERRY TOMATOES, CANNELLINI BEANS & CIDER

1 onion, finely sliced
500g cherry tomatoes
400g tin cannellini beans,
    drained and rinsed
1 tsp dried oregano
1 large tbsp Dijon mustard
3 large garlic cloves, sliced
Small bunch of thyme
200ml sweet cider
8 good-quality vegan sausages
1–2 tbsp olive oil

So this is one where I'm obviously talking about veggie sausages – and I don't mean the ones formed out of mixed veg into sausage shapes but the ones that look like sausages. I think the Linda McCartney ones are about the best, but choose for yourself.

1 Preheat the oven to 200°C/fan 180°C/gas 6.

2 This is a really simple one-pot recipe; just combine the onion, cherry tomatoes, cannellini beans, oregano, mustard, garlic, most of the bunch of thyme and the cider in the base of a small roasting tin. Lay the sausages on top of the vegetables, drizzle each with a little oil and cook for 20 minutes or until the sausages are just beginning to brown. Carefully remove the tray from the oven and turn each of the sausages over. Season the upturned side with salt and pepper then return the tin to the oven and cook for 20–25 minutes until the sausages are cooked through.

3 Serve sprinkled with the remaining thyme.

MACARONI, LEEK & PARSLEY CHEESE

300g macaroni
500g leeks, trimmed and
    cut into 1–2cm crescents
50g unsalted butter
50g plain flour
600ml semi-skimmed milk
100g mature Cheddar cheese,
    grated
3 tbsp roughly chopped
    flat-leaf parsley
2 tbsp dried breadcrumbs
Salt and freshly ground
    black pepper

Macaroni cheese, cauliflower cheese, broccoli cheese, cheesy leeks – all the same sauce. I find macaroni on its own can be a bit same old same old, so here I've pinged in some leeks, which livens it up no end. Peas would do the same if you don't like leeks.

1 Preheat the oven to 200°C/fan 180°C/gas 6.

2 Cook the pasta in a pan of boiling water for 3–4 minutes before adding the leeks to the pot and continuing to cook for a further 5 minutes. Drain the pasta and leeks and set aside.

3 Meanwhile, make the white sauce. Melt the butter in a medium pan and stir in the flour. Cook for 1 minute until thick, then, off the heat, gradually whisk in the milk, keeping the mixture smooth. Return the pan to the heat and stir constantly until thickened. Simmer for 2 minutes, remove from the heat, and add 75g of the Cheddar, the pasta and leeks. Stir through the parsley and season well before spooning into a 2-litre ovenproof dish.

4 Sprinkle the breadcrumbs and remaining cheese over the pasta and cook in the oven for 15–20 minutes until the top is crisp and golden and the sauce is gently bubbling.

VEGAN
PREP TIME: 1 HOUR 15 MINUTES
+ 30 MINUTES RESTING
COOKING TIME: 1 HOUR 10 MINUTES
SERVES 4–6

MAN-UP CARIBBEAN VEG CURRY & FRESH ROTI

FOR THE ROTI
200g self-raising flour,
  plus extra for dusting
½ tsp fine salt
2 tsp black or brown
  sesame seeds
1 tbsp vegetable oil
130ml warm water

FOR THE CURRY
3 white potatoes, peeled
  and cubed
200g baby aubergines
  or 1 large, sliced
3 tbsp olive oil
3 shallots, sliced
1 red pepper, deseeded
  and sliced
1 yellow pepper, deseeded
  and sliced
3 garlic cloves, sliced
1 Scotch bonnet chilli, halved
1 tsp allspice
1 tsp cayenne pepper
1 tsp ground coriander
2 x 400g tins full-fat
  coconut milk
½ small pineapple, peeled,
  cored and cut into cubes
3 tbsp crunchy peanut butter
Juice of 1 lime, plus extra
  wedges to serve
Small bunch of coriander,
  roughly chopped
50g coconut flakes, toasted
Salt and freshly ground
  black pepper

Go as spicy as you dare and work on your rotis – once you've got them right this is the bomb to serve anyone unsure about the veggie-vegan thing.

1 Prepare the roti. Sift the flour and salt into a large bowl and add the sesame seeds. Make a well in the centre and pour in the vegetable oil with the warm water. Stir and tip onto a clean work surface and knead for a few minutes until smooth. Place in a lightly oiled bowl, cover with a tea towel and leave for 25–30 minutes.

2 Meanwhile, start on the curry. Preheat the oven to 180°C/fan 160°C/gas 4. Bring a large pan of lightly salted water to the boil, add the potatoes and cook for 15 minutes. Drain and set aside. Place the aubergines on a roasting tray, drizzle with 2 tablespoons of the olive oil and toss together. Cook in the oven for 15–20 minutes or until soft.

3 In a casserole pot, heat the remaining oil over a medium heat. Add the shallots and cook gently for 5 minutes. Add the peppers, garlic and chilli and cook for 5 minutes. Stir through the spices and cook for a final minute. Add the potato and aubergine and pour over the coconut milk. Slowly bring to the boil, reduce to a simmer and cook, uncovered, for 20 minutes. Remove the chilli, then stir through the pineapple, peanut butter, lime juice, coriander and seasoning.

4 Divide the roti dough in to 8 and roll out into rounds on a lightly floured surface. Heat a non-stick griddle pan over a medium heat until almost smoking. Add the floured roti to the pan, one at a time. Cook for 2 minutes on each side or until puffed up and slightly charred. Serve the curry with the warm rotis, topped with toasted coconut flakes and extra lime wedges.

VEGETARIAN KEDGEREE

4 large eggs
300g basmati rice, rinsed
2 bay leaves
2 tbsp olive oil
2 medium onions, halved
   and thinly sliced
3 garlic cloves, crushed
1 green chilli, deseeded
   and thinly sliced
4 whole cardamom pods,
   lightly crushed
1 tsp coriander seeds
2 tsp turmeric powder
1 tbsp mild curry powder
80g green beans
150g baby spinach
Zest and juice of 1 large lemon
25g coriander, roughly
   chopped
1 tbsp black mustard seeds
Salt and freshly ground
   black pepper

So kedgeree is the kind of breakfast that you'd find served in big wealthy houses to the Lord of the Manor. I've got builder mates who will microwave last night's curry and rice and eat it for breakfast. Weird, right? Only they're both the same thing really, essentially kedgeree's lightly curried rice!

Traditionally made with smoked fish, this makes for a really wholesome breakfast or lunch with slow-release energy from the rice that will keep you going all day. It takes a slight change in your head as to what constitutes breakfast but give this a try – you might like this new approach to starting the day.

1 Bring a large pan of water to the boil, add the eggs and simmer for 6½ minutes. Remove with a slotted spoon and set aside in a bowl of cold water for 20 minutes. Peel the eggs and cut in half.

2 Bring a second pan of salted water to the boil, add the rice and bay leaves and cook gently for 15–20 minutes or until just cooked. Drain and set aside.

3 Heat the olive oil in a large non-stick frying pan over a medium heat. Add the onions and fry gently for 5–10 minutes or until soft and translucent. Add the garlic and cook for 1 minute. Add the chilli, cardamom, coriander seeds, turmeric and curry powder and cook for a further 2 minutes. Add the green beans to the pan with 2 tablespoons of water and cook for 5 minutes. Add the spinach and cook for 2 more minutes.

4 Stir the rice through the veg mixture and season with the lemon zest and juice and salt and pepper. Stir through half the coriander. Spoon the mixture into bowls, top each portion with 2 egg halves, a sprinkle of mustard seeds and an extra scattering of coriander.

BROCCOLI, POTATO & STILTON PIE

2 tbsp olive oil
60g butter
2 medium onions, halved
and thinly sliced
2 large garlic cloves, crushed
2 tbsp finely chopped
thyme leaves
4 tbsp plain flour
½ tbsp mustard powder
600ml vegetable stock
6 tbsp crème fraîche
150g Stilton or Shropshire blue
cheese, broken into chunks
4 large waxy potatoes,
finely sliced
600g Tenderstem broccoli
Salt and freshly ground
black pepper

The trouble with being fully vegan is the cheese, really. They haven't cracked it yet. When they make a really good Stilton then I'll consider switching totally to a vegan diet, but for one of my favourite pies in the world – and bear in mind I've been a Scotch egg and pork pie connoisseur for years – this is a proper take on the real thing.

1 Preheat the oven to 180°C/fan 160°C/gas 4.

2 Heat the oil and 20g of the butter in a large non-stick pan over a medium heat. Add the onions and fry gently for 5 minutes or until softened. Add the garlic and 1 tablespoon of the thyme and cook for a further minute. Stir in the flour and mustard powder and cook for 2 minutes. Take the pan off the heat and using a wooden spoon stir in the hot stock a little at a time until you have a smooth liquid. Return to a medium heat, bring to the boil and reduce to a simmer, cooking for 15 minutes or until the liquid has reduced and thickened a little. Remove from the heat, stir through the crème fraîche and large pieces of the cheese. Season to taste with salt and a good grind of black pepper.

3 Gently melt the remaining butter in a small saucepan over a low heat. Allow to cool down a little then pour over the sliced potatoes, along with the remaining thyme, tossing everything together. Season to taste.

4 Bring a medium pan of salted water to the boil, add the broccoli and blanch for 2 minutes. Lay the broccoli in a 20 x 30cm ovenproof dish and pour over the creamy cheese sauce. Top with the sliced potatoes and bake in the oven for 1 hour–1 hour 10 minutes or until golden brown and bubbling.

SPICED POTATO DOSA WITH ZINGY PINEAPPLE SALSA

FOR THE CURRY

500g new potatoes
2 tbsp vegetable oil
4 tbsp coconut oil
1 small onion, finely diced
3cm piece of ginger,
  peeled and grated
4 garlic cloves, crushed
¼ tsp hot chilli powder
2½ tsp mustard seeds
1 tsp ground turmeric
1 tsp cumin seeds
2 tsp garam marsala
5 green cardamom pods,
  crushed
Salt and freshly ground
  black pepper

FOR THE SALSA

1 small red onion, finely diced
Juice of 1 lime
1 red chilli, seeds in, finely
  chopped
1 small pineapple, diced
  into 1cm cubes
Small bunch of coriander,
  leaves only, finely chopped
2 tbsp extra virgin olive oil
Salt and freshly ground
  black pepper

FOR THE DOSAS

100g gram flour
100g plain flour
¼ tsp salt
½ tsp bicarbonate of soda
1 tsp vegetable oil

This is a potato pancake, really, but it's spiced and served with the most amazing pineapple salsa. I remember the first time I made my own pineapple salsa, I was like, 'Wow! Where has this been all my life?' Give it a go.

1 Start by making the curry. Preheat the oven to 190°C/fan 170°C/gas 6. Toss the potatoes in the vegetable oil, salt and pepper. Roast for 35–40 minutes until crispy and cooked through. Remove from the oven and, once cool enough to handle, cut any large potatoes in half.

2 Heat the coconut oil in a large frying pan over a medium heat and fry the onion, ginger and garlic for 5 minutes, until soft. In a small bowl, mix all the spices together and then fry for 2 minutes until golden and aromatic. Stir the softened spices through the roasted potatoes and set aside, covered with foil, until needed.

3 To make the salsa, simply mix all the ingredients together and season to taste. Set aside.

4 For the dosas, whisk the flours, salt and bicarbonate together. Whisk 300ml water in gradually until you have a smooth, thin batter. Heat the oil in a large frying pan and wipe out the excess with kitchen paper. Ladle a small amount of the batter into the pan and swirl it around so that you have a really thin crepe. Bubbles will appear all over the surface of the dosa as it is cooking. Cook over a high heat for 1 minute until golden and crispy underneath. Remove and stack on a plate until needed. Repeat until all the mixture has been used.

5 To build the dosa, spoon a portion of the potato mix into the middle of the dosa, top with salsa and enjoy.

VEGETARIAN
PREP TIME: 1 HOUR
COOKING TIME: 1 HOUR 15 MINUTES
SERVES 4–6

MUSHROOM & SWEET POTATO MASALA

700g sweet potatoes, peeled
   and cubed
50g ghee or unsalted butter
1 tbsp sunflower oil
1 tsp yellow mustard seeds
3 large onions, thinly sliced
3cm piece of ginger,
   peeled and grated
250g chestnut mushrooms,
   sliced
2 tsp ground cumin
2 tsp ground coriander
2 tsp turmeric
1 tsp hot chilli powder
½ tsp cayenne pepper
1 cinnamon stick
400g tin chopped tomatoes
400g tin coconut milk
4 heaped tbsp thick
   natural yoghurt
Small bunch of coriander, torn
Squeeze of lemon
Salt and freshly ground
   black pepper

I love a mushroom masala from my favourite curry house, and I've put in chunks of sweet potato here as I like a *sag aloo* (spinach potato bhaji) too, so here I've kinda combined the two.

1 Bring a large pan of salted water to the boil and add the potatoes, then parboil for 10 minutes. Drain and set aside.

2 Heat the ghee or butter and oil in a large casserole pot or saucepan over a high heat, add the mustard seeds and cook for 2–3 minutes or until they begin to pop. Lower the heat and add the onions with a good pinch of salt. Cook gently for 15 minutes or until beginning to turn golden brown and sticky, adding a small splash of water if the onions begin to stick.

3 Add the grated ginger and mushrooms. Stir through the cumin, coriander, turmeric, chilli powder and cayenne and cook for a further 5–7 minutes, until the mushrooms have softened. Add the cinnamon, tinned tomatoes and coconut milk to the pan along with the cubed sweet potatoes. Bring to the boil, reduce to a simmer and cook, uncovered, on a low heat for 35–40 minutes or until thickened and reduced slightly. Season to taste. Serve in deep bowls heaped with yoghurt, some torn coriander and a squeeze of lemon.

VEGAN
PREP TIME: 30 MINUTES
COOKING TIME: 1 HOUR 15 MINUTES
SERVES 4

PUMPKIN LAKSA, CRUNCHY CHICKPEAS & POMEGRANATE

400g tin chickpeas, rinsed
   and dried with kitchen paper
2 tbsp sunflower oil
1 tsp mild chilli powder
800g pumpkin, peeled
   and cubed
1 shallot, sliced
1 tsp turmeric
1 large garlic clove, crushed
1 large red chilli, sliced
   into thin rounds
1 thumb-sized piece of ginger,
   peeled and grated
2 x 400g tins coconut milk
500ml hot vegetable stock
1 lemongrass stick, bashed
200g udon noodles
2 tbsp tamarind paste
Juice of 1 lime
Salt and freshly ground
   black pepper
130g pomegranate seeds,
   to serve
½ small bunch of mint, torn,
   to serve

A laksa is a spicy noodle soup from the crossover of Malaysian and Chinese cooking. I've added some crunchy chickpeas for texture and pomegranate for zing and because my mum loved them.

1 Preheat the oven to 200°C/fan 180°C/gas 6. Toss the chickpeas with 1 tablespoon of the oil, the chilli powder and some seasoning and spread out over a baking sheet. Place in the oven for 20 minutes until golden brown and crunchy, leave to cool completely and set aside.

2 Bring a large pan of salted water to the boil, add the pumpkin and cook for 15 minutes or until tender. Set aside.

3 In a large pan, heat the remaining oil and add the shallot, cooking gently over a medium heat for 5–7 minutes or until softened. Add the turmeric, garlic, chilli and ginger and cook for a further 3 minutes. Add the coconut milk, stock and lemongrass to the pan along with the pumpkin. Cook for 15 minutes, uncovered. Add the noodles and cook for a further 15 minutes or until the noodles have softened. Remove the lemongrass, stir through the tamarind and lime. Season to taste. Bundle nests of the noodles into bowls and top up with a ladle or two of the broth. Finish with a handful of crunchy chickpeas, sweet pomegranate seeds and a few mint leaves.

VEGETARIAN
PREP TIME: 40 MINUTES
+ 30 MINUTES CHILLING
COOKING TIME: 1 HOUR
SERVES 4–6

FALAFEL WITH CREAMY GARLIC SAUCE & AVOCADO HUMMUS

450g butternut squash
   or sweet potato, peeled
   and cubed
2 tbsp olive oil
1 tsp allspice
1 tsp chilli flakes
2 tsp ground coriander
2 x 400g tins chickpeas,
   drained and rinsed
Small bunch of coriander
   leaves, chopped
3 tbsp plain flour, plus
   extra to coat
Juice of 1 small lemon
1 tsp nigella or onion seeds
5 tbsp sunflower oil
Salt and freshly ground
   black pepper

FOR THE GARLIC SAUCE
150g thick Greek yoghurt
100ml buttermilk
3 tbsp milk
1 fat garlic clove, crushed
2 tbsp finely chopped
   flat-leaf parsley

FOR THE AVOCADO HUMMUS
400g tin chickpeas,
   rinsed and drained
3 tbsp tahini paste
1 large garlic clove, crushed
Zest and juice of 1 lemon
1 large ripe avocado
1 tbsp olive oil or avocado oil

TO SERVE
4 flatbreads or wraps
4 tbsp pickled jalapenos
   (optional)

I wanted to show you that falafel don't have to taste as dry and tasteless as a cardboard bun. And the dip is a trip.

1 Preheat the oven to 200°C/fan 180°C/gas 6.

2 In a large roasting tray, toss the squash or sweet potato with the oil, allspice, chilli flakes and ground coriander. Season to taste. Place in the oven for 30 minutes or until just cooked.

3 Place 1 tin of the chickpeas, the roasted squash and half the coriander leaves in a food processor and blitz several times to create a rough-textured mixture. Transfer to a bowl and blitz the remaining chickpeas in the food processor to a coarse texture. Add to the rest of the mixture and stir through the flour, most of the remaining coriander leaves and the lemon juice. Season to taste. Form the mixture into 12 balls, flatten gently with the palm of your hand and sprinkle with the nigella seeds. Set aside in the fridge for at least 30 minutes to firm up.

4 Make the sauce. In a small bowl, combine the yoghurt, buttermilk, milk, garlic and parsley. Season to taste and set aside.

Recipe continued overleaf

Recipe continued

5 Next, make the hummus. Blitz the chickpeas, tahini, garlic and lemon zest and juice together in the small bowl of the food processor. Scoop the flesh out of the avocado, add to the chickpeas and blitz until smooth. Transfer to a bowl and stir through 2–3 tablespoons of cold water to create a dropping consistency. Transfer to a bowl and drizzle with the oil.

6 Now, return your attention to the falafel. Sprinkle some flour onto a plate and dip each falafel into it, making sure each one is evenly coated. Heat the sunflower oil in a large non-stick frying pan over a medium heat. Add the falafel and gently fry on each side for 5 minutes. Set aside on kitchen paper then transfer to a baking sheet and place in the hot oven for 10 minutes.

7 Meanwhile, warm the flatbreads in a low oven for 5 minutes. Assemble the flatbreads with the falafel, a good drizzle of the sauce, a spoonful of hummus, the remaining coriander and some pickled jalapenos, if you like.

MOROCCAN VEGETABLE NUT ROAST

2 tbsp olive oil
1 small onion, finely diced
2 garlic cloves, crushed
1 celery stick, finely diced
1 carrot, peeled and
  finely diced
1 tbsp ras el hanout
¼ tsp ground cinnamon
½ tsp ground turmeric
½ tsp chilli flakes
125g chestnut mushrooms,
  roughly chopped
400g tin chickpeas,
  drained and rinsed
2 tbsp tahini paste
1 tbsp tomato purée
110g fresh white breadcrumbs
1 medium egg, lightly beaten
Small handful of fresh flat-leaf
  parsley, roughly chopped
80g mixed nuts, roughly
  chopped
1 small courgette, sliced
  into thin strips lengthways
½ x 460g jar roasted red
  peppers, drained and
  sliced into strips
Salt and freshly ground
  black pepper

So my problem with nut roasts is they are generally too dry and are too nutty. Sounds daft, but there it is. This one, though, is fresh and moist and not ridiculously nutty

1 Grease and line a 900g loaf tin with baking parchment and preheat the oven to 180°C/fan 160°C/gas 4.

2 Heat half of the olive oil in a large frying pan and add the onion, garlic and celery. Cook over a low heat for about 10 minutes until softened thoroughly. Throw in the carrot and sauté for a further few minutes until tender.

3 Tip the ras el hanout, cinnamon, turmeric and chilli flakes into the pan and cook for a minute. Scrape this mixture into a large bowl and return the pan to a high heat, adding in the remaining tablespoon of olive oil.

4 Cook the mushrooms for 5 minutes until golden and softened and then add these to the onion mixture.

5 In a food processor, blitz the chickpeas with the tahini and 150ml water to form a paste. Add this to the mixing bowl and season well with salt and pepper. Finish the mixture by stirring in the tomato purée, breadcrumbs, egg, parsley and nuts.

6 To build the loaf, spread a layer of the chickpea mix in the bottom of the tin then cover this with a layer of the sliced courgettes. Cover the courgettes with more chickpea mix and follow with the roasted red peppers. Continue building up the layers until the loaf tin is full to the brim. Bake the loaf in the oven for 25–30 minutes until golden. Allow to cool for 5 minutes before slicing.

CHRISTMAS CHESTNUT ROAST

2 medium sweet
   potatoes, peeled
1 tbsp olive oil
2 thyme sprigs
2 x 190g packs of sage
   and onion stuffing
50g unsalted butter
200g cooked chestnuts,
   roughly chopped
70g walnuts, roughly chopped
Good handful of fresh
   cranberries
8 medium sage leaves
Salt and freshly ground
   black pepper

So if you're really going for it veggie-wise you'll be faced with a dilemma at Christmas dinner (or indeed any time you fancy a Sunday roast) what's going to be at the centre of it?

Well here's my recipe for a roast loaf – like a meat loaf with no meat or a nut roast without being full of nuts! Roast this up and serve slices with onion gravy, roast potatoes, red cabbage blanched then lightly browned in sesame oil, brussels sprout halves, roast cauliflower or broccoli and a Yorkshire pud! You will love it I promise.

This also makes a great veggie burger, served in slices with halloumi and avocado or a portobello mushroom.

1 Preheat the oven to 200°C/fan 180°C/gas 6. Cut the sweet potato into 2cm-sized cubes. Place in a roasting tray along with the olive oil and thyme. Season to taste and give everything a good shake to combine. Place in the preheated oven and roast for 30 minutes or until just cooked. Set aside.

2 Tip the dried stuffing into a large mixing bowl and add 700ml water along with half the butter. Add the chopped chestnuts and walnuts to the stuffing mixture. Fold through the cubes of sweet potato along with the cooking oils, being careful not to crush them.

Add the cranberries, combine gently and season everything generously with black pepper.

3 Line the base and sides of a 2.5 litre loaf tin and use 10g of the remaining butter to grease the bottom and sides well. Spoon the mixture into the tin, flattening the mixture down and compacting it as much as possible. Cover the top with foil and bake in the preheated oven for 50 minutes. Remove the foil and cook for a further 10 minutes. Leave to stand and cool thoroughly before turning out on to a baking tray. Reheat before serving by covering with foil and placing in a preheated oven at 180°C/fan 160°C/gas 4 for 40 minutes or until piping hot throughout.

4 Once reheated, place a small frying pan over a medium heat and melt the remaining butter, add the sage leaves and fry for 1 minute or until the sage curls up and becomes crisp. Pour the butter topping over the chestnut roast and slice into generous thick slices.

FOUR
EATS SHOOTS
AND LEAVES

SUPERFOOD SALAD WITH MISO & TAHINI DRESSING

140g rainbow kale, torn into bite-sized pieces
175g butternut squash, peeled and diced
175g sweet potato, peeled and diced
6 tbsp olive oil
1 tbsp maple syrup
2 corn on the cobs
140g Tenderstem broccoli
75g pomegranate seeds
50g pumpkin seeds
1 ripe avocado, sliced
Small bunch of coriander leaves, roughly chopped
Salt and freshly ground black pepper

FOR THE DRESSING
1 tbsp white miso paste
90ml rapeseed oil
2 tbsp tahini paste
2 tsp agave syrup
Juice of 1 lemon
1 garlic clove, grated

As a veggie, miso is your friend – it makes an easy soup and will liven up anything; tahini is your other friend, in any kind of dressing. So this is like having your friends over on a salad that's good for you.

1 Preheat the oven to 190°C/fan 170°C/gas 5.

2 In a jug, whisk together all the ingredients for the dressing. Place the kale in a large mixing bowl and toss with the dressing, then set aside while you make the rest of the salad. This helps to soften the kale.

3 Toss the butternut squash and sweet potato with half the olive oil, maple syrup, salt and pepper and roast for 20 minutes until tender. Once cooked, remove from the oven and set aside.

4 Cut the kernels off the corn cob by carefully running your knife lengthways down it. Place the corn kernels and broccoli in a roasting tray and drizzle with the remaining olive oil, salt and pepper. Roast in the same oven as the squash for 15 minutes until just charred. Remove and allow to cool slightly.

5 To assemble the salad, toss the corn through the kale and portion onto 4 plates. Layer up with the squash and sweet potato, broccoli, pomegranate seeds and pumpkin seeds. Place the avocado slices on top and sprinkle with a handful of coriander.

VEGAN
PREP TIME: 15 MINUTES
COOKING TIME: 5 MINUTES
SERVES 4–6

KALE & SESAME SALAD WITH MAPLE & GINGER DRESSING

200g kale, trimmed
3 large carrots, peeled
70g pecan nuts, roughly
    chopped
2 tbsp sesame seeds

FOR THE DRESSING
4 tbsp olive oil
2 tbsp white wine vinegar
3 tbsp maple syrup
Thumb-sized piece of ginger,
    peeled and grated
Salt and freshly ground
    black pepper

Dressings make a world of difference to veggie food – it's all about the herbs and dressings because, let's be honest, veg on their own can be pretty dull. My mum, bless her, would boil the flavour and living daylights out of every veg she came across, so I wasn't keen myself. This salad, however, is the bomb.

Greens are important; it doesn't matter who you ask – from medics to your mum or the bonkers types who think that all the issues in the world can be solved by eating broccoli – there's no doubt greens are good for you. (I've got a raft of rugby-playing mates and Devon farmers brought up on kale, mince and potatoes.)

If you're not eating greens with mince or spuds or if you've never liked them, this is the way to get some in. It's really tasty as a side salad or served with halloumi or feta to bounce it up to a lunch or dinner.

1 Bring a large saucepan of salted water to the boil and add the kale. Cook for 2–3 minutes until just tender before draining and blanching in cold water to stop the cooking process. Drain and set aside. Meanwhile, cut long ribbons of carrot using a peeler and toss together with the blanched kale in a large bowl.

2 Make the dressing by placing the oil, vinegar, maple syrup and ginger in a bowl and whisking. Season.

3 In a small frying pan over a medium heat, gently toast the nuts and sesame seeds until they are turning golden brown. Toss the kale and carrots with the dressing, spoon onto a serving plate and sprinkle over the toasted nuts and sesame seeds. Serve immediately.

RAW COURGETTE, CUCUMBER, HERB & TOMATO SALAD

2 courgettes
2 plum tomatoes, diced
    into small chunks
½ bulb fennel, very finely sliced
½ cucumber, deseeded and
    sliced in crescents
3 tbsp coriander leaves,
    finely chopped
3 tbsp basil leaves,
    finely chopped
1 tbsp poppy seeds
200g feta cheese, crumbled
    (optional)

FOR THE DRESSING
4 tbsp olive oil
2 tbsp white wine vinegar
3 tbsp maple syrup
1 small garlic clove, crushed
Salt and freshly ground
    black pepper

I have totally fallen in love with raw courgette; seriously, it's a lovely, crunchy veg and a superfood that claims to do everything – including make you more attractive! Ok, maybe not, but certainly healthier. This is tasty as a side, so try it before you decide.

1 Using a peeler or a mandolin, cut ribbons from the courgettes and put them into a large mixing bowl. Add the tomatoes, fennel and cucumber. Very gently, stir through the coriander, basil, poppy seeds and half of the feta.

2 Make the dressing by placing the oil, vinegar, maple syrup and garlic in a bowl and lightly whisking. Season to taste.

3 Spoon the dressing over the salad, decant onto a big serving platter and scatter over the remaining feta. Serve immediately.

DAKOS PANZANELLA

250g gluten-free bread,
   1–2 days old
3 beef tomatoes
1 small red onion,
   finely chopped
2 garlic cloves, crushed
60ml extra virgin olive oil
60ml red wine vinegar
1 medium cucumber, chopped
   into quarters lengthways,
   then sliced
A handful of caperberries
100g Kalamata olives, pitted
200g feta cheese, crumbled
Handful of basil and dill
   leaves, chopped
Salt and freshly ground
   black pepper

You don't cook this as much as prepare it and let it soak in. It's a salad around chunks of bread, essentially, but that description doesn't do the flavours justice once it's done.

1 Tear or cut the bread into 2–3cm chunks and put into a large bowl. Roughly chop the tomatoes, keeping all their juices, and add to the bowl with the onion and garlic. Toss lightly to combine and evenly distribute all the ingredients.

2 Mix together the olive oil and vinegar and pour over the bread and tomato mixture. Leave to sit for 20 minutes in the fridge so that all the flavours meld together.

3 Just before serving, toss through the cucumber, caperberries, olives, feta, basil and dill leaves. Season to taste and serve.

BEER-BATTERED VEG WITH GARLIC AIOLI

80g cornflour
80g plain flour
½ tsp fine salt
1 large egg, lightly beaten
190ml cold lager beer
2 large sweet potatoes,
    peeled and sliced
1 litre sunflower oil, for frying
1 large courgette, sliced
100g trimmed Tenderstem
    broccoli
1 large red pepper, sliced

FOR THE AIOLI
180g good-quality mayonnaise
1 garlic clove, grated
Zest and juice of ½ small lemon
Salt and freshly ground
    black pepper

Also called tempura veg, this is really tasty, but it is fiddly. However, it's worth it if you like it like I do. You've got to get the batter just right and the veg dry to make it stick.

1 Begin by making the batter. Sift the cornflour, flour and salt into a large mixing bowl. Make a deep well in the centre of the dry ingredients and in several additions whisk in the egg and lager to create a smooth batter. Set aside in the fridge.

2 Bring a large pan of lightly salted water to the boil. Add the sweet potato to the pan and boil for 12–15 minutes or until tender. Drain and allow to steam dry for a few minutes.

3 Heat the oil in a deep-fat fryer or tall saucepan and use a thermometer to read the temperature of the oil – you are looking for it to reach 190°C. Alternatively, drop a small cube of bread into the oil – if it turns golden brown after 30 seconds the oil is hot enough to deep-fry. Dip each of the vegetable pieces into the batter and then plunge straight into the oil. Cook all the vegetables in 2–3 batches for about 2 minutes each or until an even brown colour. Drain and set aside on kitchen paper.

4 Make the aioli by mixing the mayonnaise together with the garlic and lemon zest and juice in a small bowl. Season with salt and black pepper. Spread the crisp tempura veg onto a large sharing plate, sprinkle with sea salt and serve with the lemony aioli.

VEGETARIAN
PREP TIME: 20 MINUTES
COOKING TIME: 1 HOUR
SERVES 4–6

ROASTED SQUASH, BARLEY, CHESTNUT & FETA SALAD

1 medium squash, peeled,
   deseeded and sliced into
   4–5cm pieces
2 tbsp olive oil
½ tsp chilli flakes
100g pearl barley
1 onion, finely sliced
180g cooked whole chestnuts,
   roughly chopped
1 tbsp roughly chopped
rosemary leaves
100g feta cheese, crumbled
A handful of parsley
   leaves, picked

FOR THE DRESSING
1 garlic clove, crushed
2 tbsp olive oil
1 tbsp balsamic vinegar
1 tsp Dijon mustard
Salt and freshly ground
   black pepper

When I was a child my dad used to take me and as many kids from our estate as we could fit into our car to Osterley Park to play footie and to hunt for edible chestnuts. We'd then roast the chestnuts at home in front of the fire. You didn't get much chestnut – they were mostly burnt and so were our fingers trying to open them – but I loved them and have loved them ever since. You can now get chestnuts in the supermarket; they're wonderful in stews and salads like this one.

1 Preheat the oven to 200°C/fan 180°C/gas 6.

2 Arrange the squash over two baking trays. Drizzle 1 tablespoon of olive oil over the pieces and gently coat before sprinkling over the chilli flakes. Roast in the oven for 20–25 minutes, turning once during cooking. Remove from the oven once the squash has caramelised slightly.

3 Bring a medium pot of water to the boil and add the barley. Bring back to a boil, then cover the pot and reduce the heat to low. Simmer for 20–25 minutes, or until the grains are soft. Drain any excess water and set aside.

Recipe continued overleaf

Recipe continued

4 Meanwhile, heat the remaining oil in a frying pan over a high heat. Add the onion and fry for 2–3 minutes, until softened, before stirring through the chestnuts and rosemary. Continue to cook for a further 3–4 minutes.

5 Make the dressing by combining the garlic, olive oil, balsamic vinegar and Dijon mustard. Season to taste.

6 Place the squash crescents in a large mixing bowl and add the barley, fried onion and chestnuts. Add the parsley leaves and half the crumbled feta. Pour over the dressing and, very gently, mix with your hands until the ingredients are combined. Serve, topped with the remaining feta.

BATTATA HARA

800g new potatoes
3 tbsp olive oil
½ head garlic, cloves separated
　but left unpeeled
2 red peppers, deseeded
　and sliced into 1cm strips
2 large tomatoes, chopped
　into 2cm chunks
1 medium red chilli, deseeded
　and finely chopped
½ tsp cayenne pepper
½ tsp ground coriander
1 tsp ground cumin
25g coriander leaves,
　roughly chopped
Juice and zest of ½ lemon
Salt and freshly ground
　black pepper

TO SERVE
1 garlic clove, crushed
100g thick natural yoghurt

These are essentially little toasty potatoes with extra flavour, but that's a bit like saying Usain Bolt is a runner! Lebanese in origin, these are just great as a side dish but I could sit and eat a plate of them on their own.

1 Preheat the oven to 200°C/fan 180°C/gas 6.

2 Bring a large pan of salted water to the boil. Add the new potatoes and cook for 5 minutes. Drain and allow to steam dry for a further 5 minutes. Slice each potato in half and place in a large roasting tin with the oil, garlic cloves, red peppers, tomatoes and chilli. Sprinkle with the cayenne, ground coriander and ground cumin and season to taste.

3 Toss everything together one last time before placing in the oven to roast for 40–45 minutes or until the potato skins are golden brown and crispy. Once cooked, stir through the coriander leaves and squeeze over the lemon juice and a little zest.

4 Stir the crushed garlic into the yoghurt and serve alongside the potatoes.

ROASTED CARROTS WITH TOASTED COUSCOUS, CHICKPEAS & HERBY CRÈME FRAÎCHE

500g baby Chantenay carrots,
  tops trimmed
1½ tbsp cumin seeds
½ tbsp cayenne pepper
1 tsp turmeric
3 tbsp rapeseed oil
1 whole preserved lemon,
  cut in half
1½ tbsp clear runny honey
250g couscous
250ml hot vegetable stock
400g tin chickpeas, drained
  and rinsed
60g flaked almonds, toasted
Zest and juice of 1 large lemon
½ small bunch of dill, torn
Salt and freshly ground
  black pepper

HERBY CRÈME FRAÎCHE
150g crème fraîche
2 tbsp finely chopped dill
2 tbsp finely chopped mint
2 tbsp whole milk
Sea salt and freshly ground
  black pepper

Couscous is another ingredient that I could take or leave, as it's rarely done well. If you're preparing couscous as a side dish, mix in the herbs the night before and cover the bowl with cling film, then the next day add the boiling water, cover in cling film again and walk away. That's how you do tasty couscous. However, here we are toasting it first, which tastes great with the carrots, which are too good to be true.

1 Heat the oven to 200°C/fan 180°C/gas 6. Throw the carrots into a large roasting tray and toss with the cumin seeds, cayenne pepper, turmeric, 2 tablespoons of the oil and the preserved lemon. Season to taste and roast in the oven for 25 minutes. Pull out of the oven and drizzle over the honey. Reduce the oven temperature to 180°C/fan 160°C/gas 4, return to the oven for a further 10 minutes until the carrots are tender and roasted. Discard the preserved lemons and set the carrots aside to cool a little.

2 Heat a large non-stick frying pan over a medium heat. Add the couscous to the pan and toast gently for 5–7 minutes or until the grains are a toasted, golden brown colour, shaking the pan occasionally. Tip into a large bowl, pour over the stock, fluff up with a fork and cover with a plate for 10 minutes or until all the water is nicely absorbed. Stir through the remaining 1 tablespoon of oil and set aside.

3 In a small bowl, combine the crème fraîche, dill, mint, zest from the lemon for the couscous and milk. Add a little more milk if the crème fraiche dressing is too thick – it should be a slightly thicker consistency than double cream. Season with the salt and a little black pepper.

4 Place the chickpeas and ½ tablespoon of water in a small saucepan over a low heat and gently warm the chickpeas through for 5 minutes, stirring halfway. In a large bowl, use your hands to toss together the cooled carrots and toasted couscous. Drizzle in any remaining cooking juices or spices from the carrots. Stir through half the flaked almonds and the chickpeas as well as the lemon juice. Season to taste. Pile the mixture onto a large sharing plate, top with any remaining toasted almonds and the torn dill. Finally, serve with the creamy crème fraîche dressing.

ASIAN SLAW

120g vermicelli noodles
   (also known as glass noodles)
½ head sweetheart cabbage,
   very finely sliced
¼ small head red cabbage,
   very finely sliced
60g mangetout, sliced
   on the diagonal
1 large green chilli, deseeded
   and finely chopped
6 small spring onions,
   finely sliced
150g salted, roasted peanuts,
   roughly chopped
Large bunch of mint, roughly
   chopped, to serve

FOR THE DRESSING
2 garlic cloves, finely chopped
2 tbsp fish sauce
1 tbsp caster sugar
Juice and zest of 2 limes

Zingy, fresh and tasty, this is simply a great fresh salad with a hint of Thailand, but it makes you look like you know what you're doing around a kitchen, even if you're just following the instructions. You'll be asked to be a judge on Great British Menu after you've knocked this one up for others. Keep the ends of your fingers tucked back when you're chopping these ingredients, otherwise it'll be Asian chainSlaw finger massacre!

1 Start by soaking the noodles in boiling water for 3–4 minutes. Drain and run under cool water until the noodles separate. A trick I've learnt is to take scissors to your noodles at this point, cutting them into shorter lengths; scissors are the most efficient utensil for making the noodles a little more manageable to eat.

2 Meanwhile, make the dressing by combining all the ingredients. Allow it to sit for a few minutes, if you have the time – the garlic will infuse with the lime juice and it will taste all the better.

3 Next, put all the remaining ingredients in a large bowl (reserve a few peanuts for decoration). Pour over the dressing and use a 'lifting' motion to make sure the whole salad is dressed.

4 Serve scattered with the chopped mint and the reserved peanuts sprinkled on top.

VEGAN
PREP TIME: 20 MINUTES
COOKING TIME: 15 MINUTES
SERVES 6

BRIGHT & NUTTY QUINOA SALAD WITH BASIL OIL

250g dried mixed quinoa
160g frozen edamame beans
2 tbsp rapeseed oil
30g pistachios, roughly
    chopped
30g hazelnuts, roughly chopped
2 medium ripe avocados, diced
125g radishes, cut in half
½ cucumber, thinly sliced
    into crescents
1 small pomegranate,
    seeds only
1 small bunch of chives,
    chopped
1 tbsp poppy seeds
2 tbsp parsley, roughly chopped
Salt and freshly ground
    black pepper

FOR THE BASIL OIL
2 handfuls of basil leaves
1 small garlic clove, cut in half
50–75ml olive oil
Juice of ½ lemon
Salt and freshly ground
    black pepper

Everyone's talking about quinoa at the moment (pronounced 'keen wah', by the way) but, like couscous, you've got to work to make it tasty. Here's my nutty version of a quinoa salad. Remember, chaps, hazelnuts are supposed to ward off prostate problems. Ever heard of a squirrel with prostate trouble? Well, there you go. I also like to include chestnuts in mine, but they're not to everyone's taste.

1 Start with the quinoa. Bring 500ml salted water to the boil, tip in the quinoa and cook for about 12 minutes, then add the edamame for the final minute of cooking. Drain and transfer to a large mixing bowl, tossing with the rapeseed oil. Set aside to cool.

2 Place a small frying pan over a medium heat. Add both nuts to the pan and lightly toast for a few minutes until they are turning a light golden brown. Set aside.

3 Make the basil oil by putting two-thirds of the basil leaves in a mini food processor with half a garlic clove, a generous pour of oil and a good pinch of sea salt. Blitz or pound to form a rough, sludgy purée, adding more oil if it needs loosening further. Stir in a few drops of lemon juice to brighten, then taste and adjust the seasoning. If you like, strain the oil to remove the large pieces of basil leaves or just leave it rustic.

4 Combine half the basil oil with the grains, half the nuts, avocado, radishes, cucumber, half the pomegranate seeds, the chives and the poppy seeds. Season to taste. Spoon generous heaps of the salad onto a sharing plate and drizzle over the remaining dressing. Top with the remaining pomegranate seeds, nuts and roughly chopped parsley.

RAW WINTER SLAW WITH TAHINI LEMON DRESSING

FOR THE DRESSING
4 tbsp Greek yoghurt
2 tbsp tahini paste
2 tbsp lemon juice
1 fat garlic clove, crushed

FOR THE SALAD
500g celeriac, peeled and
   coarsely shredded
1 tbsp lemon juice
2 medium carrots,
   coarsely grated
1 small sweetheart cabbage,
   finely sliced
A handful of radishes,
   finely sliced
25g flat-leaf parsley leaves,
   roughly chopped
25g mint leaves, roughly
   chopped
Salt and freshly ground
   black pepper
Parmesan, to serve

Tahini is what you put with chickpeas to make hummus, but on its own it can be your friend in dressings that will make boring salads interesting. This lemon one is great on the raw root vegetables here.

1 To make the dressing, mix all the ingredients together and set aside.

2 Squeeze the lemon juice over the celeriac to prevent it discolouring. Combine with all of the remaining vegetables in a large bowl.

3 Pour the yoghurty dressing over the salad, scatter over the freshly chopped herbs and season with freshly ground black pepper and salt. Just before serving, toss everything together. Shave the Parmesan using a vegetable peeler and scatter over the salad to serve.

VEGETARIAN
PREP TIME: 25 MINUTES
COOKING TIME: 5 MINUTES
SERVES 6

WATERMELON, HAZELNUT, FETA, TOMATO & HERB SALAD

1 medium watermelon
250g large tomatoes, quartered
150g feta cheese, crumbled
   into large pieces
½ small bunch of basil,
   roughly chopped
½ small bunch of mint,
   roughly chopped
60g hazelnuts, chopped

FOR THE DRESSING
50ml olive oil
50ml white wine vinegar
½ tbsp poppy seeds
Salt and freshly ground
   black pepper

I know i need to develop a relationship with salad every now and again as I get older. Just like how you need to have a relationship with your doctor for certain health checks, they're both slightly uncomfortable relationships, for guys in particular. I can't quite put my finger on why – maybe it's because he can… Anyway, here's a salad that's enjoyable no matter what the company, and like an apple a day it should keep the doctor away a little longer.

1 Cut the watermelon into thick rounds and slice each round into quarters. Lay on a large serving plate.

2 Make the dressing. Whisk together the olive oil, vinegar and poppy seeds. Season to taste.

3 Toss together the tomatoes, feta cheese, herbs and dressing. Arrange together on the plate with the chunks of watermelon.

4 Heat a small dry frying pan over a medium heat and gently toast the chopped hazelnuts for 2 minutes or until starting to turn lightly browned. Scatter the warm hazelnuts over the salad. Serve immediately.

FIVE

A BIT ON
THE SIDE

VEGAN
PREP TIME: 15 MINUTES
COOKING TIME: 45 MINUTES
SERVES 4

SWEET POTATO & BLACK BEAN NACHOS WITH GREEN CHILLI SALSA

FOR THE NACHOS

1 medium sweet potato, peeled and diced into 5cm chunks
¼ tsp ground coriander
½ tsp smoked paprika
2 tbsp olive oil
1 small onion, finely diced
1 garlic clove, crushed
400g tin black beans, drained and rinsed
Small bunch of fresh coriander, finely chopped, plus extra for serving
1 red chilli, finely sliced
150g tortilla chips
Salt and freshly ground black pepper

FOR THE SALSA

1 green pepper, deseeded and quartered
1 green chilli
1 small red onion, quartered
1 cucumber, deseeded
2 tbsp olive oil
Juice of 1 lime
1 tbsp agave nectar or honey
Small handful of coriander leaves
Salt and freshly ground black pepper

It's a sharing plate until you taste it, then it's just for you in front of the sport or a movie.

1 Preheat the oven to 190°C/fan 170°C/gas 5.

2 Throw the sweet potato into a mixing bowl along with the ground coriander, paprika, 1 tablespoon of the olive oil, salt and pepper. Spread onto a foil-lined baking tray and roast in the oven for 25–30 minutes until they are soft all the way through.

3 Meanwhile, heat the remaining olive oil in a small saucepan and cook the onion and garlic on a medium heat until softened and slightly browned. Throw in the black beans, coriander (stalks, leaves and all), red chilli and 80ml water, stirring well. Bring to a simmer and cook for 10 minutes. Lightly crush the black beans with the back of a wooden spoon, take the pan off the heat and leave to one side.

4 For the salsa, simply blitz the pepper, chilli, red onion, cucumber, olive oil, lime juice and agave together in a food processor and season with salt and pepper to taste. You should have a tasty, bright green salsa with a good, thick consistency.

5 Check the sweet potatoes are cooked through and, if so, lightly crush with the back of a fork.

6 To build the nachos, simply spread the tortilla chips on a platter and load up with the spiced sweet potato, black beans and salsa, topping with a generous handful of freshly chopped coriander.

FRIED POTATOES WITH GARLIC, GREEN CHILLI & CORIANDER

800g large floury potatoes
100g butter
2 tbsp olive oil
4 fat garlic cloves,
   lightly bashed
1 tsp ground coriander
1 tsp cumin seeds
2 medium green chillies,
   halved and thinly sliced
Juice of ½ lemon
25g coriander leaves, torn
Salt and freshly ground
   black pepper

This is just great. I could blather on for ages about why it's great, but just make it, then plonk yourself down in front of the telly and some sport and eat a bowl of it and tell me it's not great. Go on, I dare you!

1 Bring a large pan of salted water to the boil. Add the potatoes and boil for 15 minutes or until a cutlery knife is easily inserted. Allowed to steam dry. Once the potatoes are cool to the touch, peel off the skins and cut into large chunks.

2 Heat half the butter and the olive oil in a large frying pan over a medium heat until foaming. Add the potatoes to the pan with the garlic cloves, sprinkle over the ground coriander and cumin and fry on a low–medium heat for 15 minutes, gradually adding the remaining butter and turning the potatoes regularly until golden brown and crispy.

3 Sprinkle over the sliced chillies; squeeze the lemon juice over the potatoes and season to taste. Serve with a generous scattering of coriander leaves.

VEGETARIAN
PREP TIME: 10 MINUTES
COOKING TIME: 30 MINUTES
SERVES 6

SMOKY SWEET POTATO FRIES WITH LEMON & GARLIC MAYO

FOR THE FRIES
800g (about 3 large) sweet
   potatoes, peeled
2 tbsp extra virgin olive oil
2½ tsp smoked paprika
½ tsp ground coriander
50g fine polenta
Salt and freshly ground
   black pepper

FOR THE MAYO
250g mayonnaise
1 garlic clove, crushed
Zest of 1 lemon, juice
   of ½ lemon
Small handful of flat leaf
   parsley, leaves picked
   and finely chopped
Salt and freshly ground
   black pepper

Sweet potatoes are good for you and there's no arguing the point that if you're health conscious and you want to eat a potato, a sweet one is the way to go.

But beware, someone like me doesn't want to overtrain, to look too fit, pumped up, sport a washboard six pack, etc, as let's face it it can be intimidating to others. So I offset a healthy sweet potato with a lemon and garlic mayo – for the sake of others, you understand? Not just because it's seriously lovely.

1 Preheat the oven to 190°C/fan 170°C/gas 5. Chop the sweet potatoes into 1cm-wide chips and put in a bowl with the olive oil, smoked paprika and ground coriander. Toss the chips to coat and season with salt and pepper.

2 Add the polenta to the bowl and mix again, making sure all the fries are well coated in the crumb. Spread the fries onto a foil lined baking tray and bake in the oven for 12–14 minutes, then turn them over and cook for a further 12–14 minutes. Remove from the oven when the fries are crispy and slightly golden.

3 Meanwhile, make the mayo by mixing together the mayonnaise, garlic, lemon zest and juice, chopped parsley and some salt and pepper. Serve the fries piled high with a bowl of mayo on the side.

MAKE IT VEGAN
You can make this a vegan version
if you use vegan mayonnaise instead.

RICH BLACK BEAN, SPINACH & CHEDDAR QUESADILLA

1 tbsp olive oil
1 shallot, finely chopped
1 garlic clove, crushed
1 tsp smoked paprika
1 tsp ground coriander
200g chopped tomatoes
1 heaped tsp soft brown sugar
400g tin black beans,
    drained and rinsed
2 tbsp coriander leaves,
    roughly chopped
4 large flour tortillas
40g baby spinach
75g strong Cheddar cheese,
    finely grated
Salt and freshly ground
    black pepper

Black beans, spinach and Cheddar – a handful of heaven. It's snack time Mexican-style.

1 Warm the olive oil in a shallow pan and cook the shallot over a gentle heat until just soft. Stir through the garlic and continue to sauté for a further minute before adding the spices and frying until they release their aroma, roughly 2–3 minutes. Pour over the tomatoes and sugar. Taste and adjust the seasoning with salt and black pepper. Spoon the beans into the mixture and cook, uncovered for 8–10 minutes, until any excess liquid has all but disappeared and you are left with quite a thick, rich filling. Gently stir through half the coriander.

2 Heat a frying pan large enough to hold your tortilla. Once hot, place a tortilla in the bottom of the pan (no oil needed) and spoon over half of the bean mixture. Top with half of the spinach leaves and sprinkle with half the Cheddar. Sandwich with another tortilla and cook over a medium heat until the tortilla starts to turn golden, 4–5 minutes. Flip the tortilla over and cook the other side for a further 3–4 minutes. Slide onto a board and cut into triangles. Cook the other tortillas in the same way and eat immediately.

VEGAN
PREP TIME: 20 MINUTES
COOKING TIME: 45 MINUTES
SERVES 4

ROASTED CAULIFLOWER AND PORTOBELLO MUSHROOMS

1 large head cauliflower, trimmed and broken into florets
1 red onion, cut into wedges
200g portobello mushrooms, thickly sliced
3 tbsp rapeseed or olive oil
1½ tsp ground turmeric
1 tsp cumin seeds
50g hazelnuts, skin on, roughly chopped
2 garlic cloves, crushed
2–3 tbsp parsley, roughly chopped
2–3 tbsp dill, roughly chopped
Juice of ½ small lemon
Salt and freshly ground black pepper

I honestly thought cauliflower sucked when people went on about it, but roast it until the ends go brown and it's a different creature; nutty and flavoursome. In this recipe, even the humble mushroom emerges from the oven as a meaty little treat.

1 Preheat the oven to 180°C/fan 160°C/gas 4.

2 In a large roasting tray, toss together the cauliflower, onion wedges, mushrooms, oil, turmeric and cumin seeds and season to taste. Roast for 35–40 minutes or until the cauliflower is tender and turning golden brown.

3 Add the hazelnuts and garlic to the tray, toss to combine and cook for a further 5 minutes.

4 Just before serving, toss the soft herbs through the veg mix and squeeze over the lemon juice.

VEGETARIAN
PREP TIME: 5 MINUTES
COOKING TIME: 20 MINUTES
SERVES 4

GARLIC PORTOBELLO MUSHROOMS

8 portobello mushrooms,
  cleaned
1–2 tbsp garlic paste
20g butter
4 tbsp dried breadcrumbs
2 tbsp olive oil

Everyone likes a garlic mushroom – it's a top snack and easier to do than falling off a log. Talking of logs, do you know you can order logs on the internet that are impregnated with mushrooms? You drop them in a bath of water and keep them in a cool, dark shed, then you can harvest mushrooms when you want. Cool, eh?

1 Preheat the oven to 200°C/fan 180°C/gas 6.

2 Place the mushrooms, stalks facing upwards, on a baking tray and squeeze a small bit of garlic paste in the centre of each. Add a knob of butter and finish with a sprinkling of breadcrumbs.

3 Drizzle with olive oil and roast for 20 minutes.

VEGAN
PREP TIME: 15 MINUTES
COOKING TIME: 1 HOUR 10 MINUTES
SERVES 4–6

MARMITE ROAST POTATOES

4 tbsp olive oil
1.5kg Maris Piper potatoes,
   peeled and quartered
3 tbsp Marmite

My lovely friend Sammy Jo told me about this idea and I've been making these potatoes ever since. A roast potato is a wonderful thing, in fact a spud is a wondrous thing in general when you think of its versatility – chips, dauphinoise, gratin, sauté, jacket. My mate Julian wants to open potato world with rides and merchandise, but he's bonkers. Marmite roasts, though? Now we're talking!

1 Preheat the oven to 180°C/fan 160°C/gas 4. Pour 3 tablespoons of the oil into a large roasting tray and put it in the oven to heat up while you cook the potatoes.

2 Bring a large pan of salted water to the boil and cook the potatoes for 7–8 minutes. Drain them through a colander and toss roughly to fluff up the outsides of the potatoes, then allow them to stream dry for a few minutes. Tip the potatoes into the tray with the hot oil, toss gently in the oil and roast for 40 minutes.

3 Turn up the oven temperature to 200°C/fan 180°C/gas 6. In a bowl, combine the remaining 1 tablespoon of oil with the Marmite and gently whisk together with a fork. Pull the cooked potatoes out of the oven and toss with the Marmite mixture, then return to the oven for a final 15–20 minutes until they are crispy.

VEGAN
PREP TIME: 15 MINUTES
COOKING TIME: 15 MINUTES
SERVES 6 AS A SIDE

GRIDDLED SWEET POTATOES WITH CHILLI, MINT & GARLIC

2 large sweet potatoes, peeled and cut into 1cm slices
2–3 tbsp sunflower oil
Salt and freshly ground black pepper

FOR THE DRESSING
1 small red chilli, deseeded and finely chopped
3 tbsp finely chopped mint leaves
2 small garlic cloves, crushed
3–4 tbsp olive oil

I've said it before and here I go again. Sweet potato is the food of athletes, body builders and champions, but it's important not to overtrain and be too pumped up, so take a moment to lay back on the sofa and enjoy this dish.

1 Brush the sweet potato slices with oil to coat them all over and season generously with salt. Preheat a griddle pan until smoking hot then lie the sweet potato slices straight onto the griddle. Don't overcrowd the pan, as this will only steam the sweet potato. Griddle the potato slices for 3–4 minutes on each side, before turning over and repeating.

2 Make the dressing by simply combining the chilli, mint, garlic and olive oil. Arrange the sweet potato slices onto a platter and spoon over the dressing. Season and serve immediately.

CHEESE AND CUMIN MASH

900g Maris Piper potatoes,
  peeled and quartered
80ml rapeseed oil
2½ tsp cumin seeds
80g Gouda or extra-mature
  Cheddar cheese, grated
Salt and freshly ground
  black pepper

We all know cheesy mash – cumin just gives it an edge. Give it a try.

1 Bring a large pan of salted water to the boil. Add the potatoes and cook for 15–20 minutes or until a cutlery knife can be easily inserted into the potatoes. Drain through a colander and allow to steam dry for 5 minutes. Pass through a potato ricer back into the pan or mash until smooth.

2 In a small frying pan, heat the rapeseed oil, add the cumin seeds and cook for 3 minutes or until popping. Pour the cumin seeds and hot rapeseed oil into the mash along with the grated cheese, then fold everything together gently to combine. Season generously with salt and pepper.

VEGETARIAN
PREP TIME: 1 HOUR
+ 45 MINUTES RISING
COOKING TIME: 20 MINUTES
SERVES 6

SPINACH & CHEESE MIDDLE EASTERN FLATBREADS – GOZLEME

FOR THE FLATBREADS

300g plain flour, plus extra
    for dusting
1 x 7g sachet fast-action
    dried yeast
¼ tsp salt
3 tbsp extra virgin olive oil,
    plus extra for drizzling
1 tbsp runny honey
300ml warm water

FOR THE FILLING

3 tbsp olive oil
2 banana shallots, finely diced
1 garlic clove, crushed
260g baby spinach
100g feta cheese
250g ricotta cheese
¼ whole nutmeg, grated
Zest of 1 lemon
1½ tsp dried oregano
Salt and freshly ground
    black pepper

Middle Eastern cooking has some real delights – hence the whole Turkish thing, I guess. Anyway, I had a girlfriend when I was 20 whose mum made these. It kept the relationship going far longer than it deserved…

1 To make the flatbreads, mix together the flour, yeast, salt, olive oil and honey with a cutlery knife. Gradually stir in the water until you have a rough dough. Turn out onto a floured surface and knead for 5–8 minutes until smooth and elastic. Lightly grease a clean bowl with olive oil and add the dough, then cover with cling film and leave in a warm place for 45 minutes until risen and doubled in size.

2 Now make the filling. Add the olive oil to a large, deep frying pan and heat over a medium–high heat. Add the shallots and sauté, for 8–10 minutes, until soft, adding the garlic for the final minute. Set aside.

3 Meanwhile, empty the spinach into a colander or sieve and pour over a kettle's worth of boiling water. The spinach will wilt under the heat. Empty the spinach onto a clean tea towel and roll and squeeze out any excess water. Roughly chop the spinach and add it into the shallot bowl. Crumble over the feta and ricotta and mix into the spinach with the nutmeg, lemon zest, oregano and some salt and pepper and set aside.

4 Scrape out the dough into an oiled surface and divide into 6 equal pieces. Using your hands, stretch each piece of dough into a rectangle about 15 x 20cm. Spread one end of each flatbread with one-sixth of the spinach filling, leaving a centimetre border. Fold over the other side and pinch the edges to seal them.

5 Heat a large, dry frying pan over a high heat. Cook the flatbreads one or two at a time for about 3 minutes on each side until golden and crispy. Remove to a chopping board, slice in half and enjoy.

CUMIN & PINE NUT HUMMUS

400g tin chickpeas, drained
   and rinsed
3 tbsp tahini paste
1 large garlic clove, crushed
2 tbsp olive oil, plus a drizzle
   to serve
Zest and juice of 1 lemon
40g pine nuts
1 tsp cumin seeds
Salt and freshly ground
   black pepper

You can eat pretty much any veg dipped in hummus, and if you can make your own – even better! My brother John makes a top hummus, and here's a lovely one for you to try.

1 Blitz the chickpeas, tahini paste, garlic, olive oil and lemon zest and juice together in a food processor until smooth. Transfer to a bowl and stir through 3–4 tablespoons of cold water to create a dropping consistency. Season to taste.

2 Heat a small frying pan until hot and add the pine nuts and cumin seeds. Toast over a medium heat for 2–3 minutes until the nuts are golden. Sprinkle over the hummus and top with a drizzle of olive oil.

MIDDLE EASTERN BLACK RICE SALAD

200ml red wine vinegar
1 tbsp runny honey or
 agave nectar
1 small red onion, very finely
 sliced into half moons
200g black rice
1 small cucumber, deseeded
 and sliced on an angle
3 spring onions, finely sliced
 on an angle
150g cherry tomatoes, halved
50g flaked almonds
Small bunch of coriander
 leaves, roughly chopped
Small bunch of mint leaves,
 roughly chopped

FOR THE DRESSING
2 tsp cumin seeds
65ml extra virgin olive oil
1 tbsp runny honey
1½ tsp za'atar
Juice of 1 lemon
2 tbsp pomegranate molasses
Salt and freshly ground
 black pepper

Black rice is an acquired taste, but this recipe will help you acquire it. Honey, cumin, mint and coriander all combine to delight.

1 In a small bowl, mix together the vinegar and honey or agave nectar. Stir in the red onion and leave to gently pickle.

2 Rinse the rice in a sieve until the water runs clear. Bring 1.5 litres of salted water to the boil in a large saucepan and tip in the rice. Boil for 30–35 minutes until al dente. Once cooked, drain through a sieve and rinse under cold running water until cool. Empty into a large mixing bowl and add the cucumber, spring onions and tomatoes.

3 Next prepare the seeds for the dressing. In a dry frying pan, toast the cumin seeds over a low heat for 2–3 minutes until they start to smell aromatic. Then pour into a pestle and mortar and lightly grind. In the same pan, toast the almonds over a low heat for another 2-3 minutes until they start to turn golden. Set aside. Pour the cumin seeds out into a small bowl or jug, add the olive oil and runny honey and stir to combine. Add all of the remaining dressing ingredients to the jug and whisk together. Set aside.

4 Pour the dressing through the salad and stir through the fresh herbs and toasted almonds. Drain the onions from their pickling liquid and arrange them on the top of the salad before serving.

CHARGRILLED CORN WITH CHILLI & CORIANDER BUTTER

100g butter, softened
½ red chilli, deseeded
   and finely chopped
Zest of 1 lime
2 tbsp coriander leaves,
   chopped
4 sweetcorn cobs, husks
   removed
A little olive oil, for brushing
Salt and freshly ground
   black pepper

This is the Formula 1 of corn on the cob. Get that herbed butter on and get your laughing gear round that corn. Hmmm…

1 In a small bowl, mash the softened butter, red chilli, lime zest, coriander and a good grind of pepper until smooth. Chill until needed.

2 Brush the cobs with olive oil and cook for 15 minutes on a hot griddle pan or barbecue grill, turning occasionally to ensure even cooking. Slather with the chilli and lime butter and serve, sprinkled with a little salt and black pepper.

VEGAN
PREP TIME: 10 MINUTES
COOKING TIME: 35 MINUTES
SERVES 6

BAKED SALTY MISO AUBERGINES

4 medium aubergines
3 tbsp sesame oil
2–3 tbsp white miso paste
1 tbsp hot water
2 tbsp sesame seeds, toasted
8 spring onions,
   sliced diagonally
1 red chilli, deseeded
   and thinly sliced
Salt and freshly ground
   black pepper

I make this all the time as a snack. My 22-year-old son Charles said, 'Dad, I'll try anything, but aubergines suck – apart from in melanzane parmigiana'. I made him this and he loved it.

1 Preheat the oven to 200°C/fan 180°C/gas 6. Cut the aubergines in half lengthways, slicing straight down the stalk, keeping it attached. Using a small sharp knife, cut a criss-cross pattern in the flesh. Place the aubergine halves on a large baking tray and drizzle with the sesame oil. Mix the miso paste with the hot water to loosen the texture, then spread it over each aubergine, sprinkling them with sesame seeds. Season well and place in the oven for 30–35 minutes until the flesh is soft and creamy. Keep an eye on the aubergines and if they are burning, simply cover with foil to prevent the flesh becoming too black.

2 Transfer the aubergine halves to a large plate and top with the spring onions and red chilli. Serve as a side dish or as a main with a peppery salad.

STIR-FRIED BUTTERNUT SQUASH WITH CHILLI & THAI BASIL

Juice of 1 lime
2 tbsp fish sauce
1 tbsp oyster sauce
1 tbsp runny honey
2 tsp tamarind paste
2 tbsp vegetable oil
1 banana shallot, sliced
    finely into half moons
300g butternut squash,
    peeled and cut into thin
    0.5–1cm batons
3cm piece of ginger,
    peeled and grated
2 garlic cloves, crushed
1 red chilli, seeds in,
    finely chopped
Small bunch of Thai basil,
    leaves picked and
    finely chopped

It's a stir-fry and it's got butternut squash at its heart. Healthy, hearty and fresh.

1 In a small bowl, mix together the lime, fish sauce, oyster sauce, honey and tamarind paste. Set aside.

2 Heat the oil in a large frying pan. Carefully add the shallot to the pan and fry on a high heat for 1 minute before adding the butternut squash and continuing to cook for 2–3 minutes. Stir through the ginger, garlic and chilli and cook for a further minute. Add the fish sauce mixture along with a splash of water. Cover the pan with a lid and allow the squash to steam over a high heat for 2–3 minutes, until just tender. Remove from the heat and allow to sit for a minute, before stirring through the basil. Serve immediately.

VEGETARIAN
PREP TIME: 10 MINUTES
COOKING TIME: 5 MINUTES
SERVES 4 AS A SIDE DISH

CANNELLINI & FRENCH BEAN SALAD WITH ASIAN SESAME DRESSING

400g tin cannellini beans,
    drained and rinsed
200g French beans
2 spring onions, sliced
    thinly on the diagonal
Small handful of mint, leaves
    picked and roughly chopped
Small handful of coriander,
    leaves picked and roughly
    chopped

FOR THE DRESSING
4 tbsp rapeseed oil
1½ tbsp rice wine vinegar
    or white wine vinegar
Juice and zest of 1 lime
2cm piece of ginger, peeled
    and finely grated
½ tsp toasted sesame oil
25g black sesame seeds
    or nigella seeds
2½ tsp agave nectar or honey
Pinch of salt

These Asian flavours are so delicious it's ridiculous. Get those healthy beans down your Gregory Peck as a tasty side.

1 In a large bowl, mix together all the ingredients for the dressing. Tip in the cannellini beans, toss to coat, then leave to marinate while you prepare the other elements of the salad.

2 Bring a large pan of lightly salted water to the boil. Add the French beans to the boiling water and cook for 2–3 minutes, until just tender. Drain, then transfer to a bowl of iced water for a further few minutes. (This stops the cooking process and helps the beans to retain some green colour.) Drain and leave to dry on some kitchen paper.

3 Add the French beans to the cannellini beans in the dressing bowl, along with the spring onions, mint and coriander leaves. Toss everything together well and serve immediately.

SIX
GUILTY
PLEASURES

RAW CHUNKY CHERRY & ALMOND FLAPJACKS

3 tbsp vegetable oil,
  plus extra for greasing
100g pitted dates
100g soft dried apricots
2 small ripe bananas
1 small apple, peeled
  and cubed
100g runny honey
200g rolled oats
150g pinhead oats or oatmeal
½ tsp salt
½ tsp almond extract
50g dried cherries
60g whole almonds
30g flaked almonds

Flapjacks, once you've worked them out, are easy and you can make them with whatever you fancy. Here's the old tried-and-trusted cherry and almond version, which is a nice treat to put in your lunch box or have with a cup of fruit tea of an evening. You may laugh, but when I do a tea run on a building site these days you'd be amazed at how many of the lads want a fruit or chamomile or green tea. What's the world coming to?!

1 Lightly grease a 20cm square tin with oil and line with baking parchment.

2 Place the dates, apricots, bananas, apple, honey and oil in a food processor and blitz everything to a smooth paste with 1 tablespoon of water.

3 In a large bowl, combine both the oats with the paste, salt and almond extract. Stir through the cherries and half the whole almonds. Spoon into the baking tin and smooth over, then sprinkle over the remaining whole and flaked almonds and leave to set in the fridge for at least 1 hour. Once chilled, slice into 12 squares. This will keep in the fridge for up to 2 days.

VEGETARIAN
PREP TIME: 15 MINUTES
+ 3½ HOURS CHILLING
NO COOKING TIME
SERVES 6–8

WHITE CHOCOLATE & RASPBERRY CHEESECAKE

Sunflower oil, for greasing
200g ginger oat biscuits
60g unsalted butter, melted
1 piece of stem ginger in syrup,
   roughly chopped
400g white chocolate
200ml double cream
500g soft cream cheese
30g icing sugar, sifted
Zest of 2 lemons
200g raspberries
30g pumpkin seeds,
   to decorate

It's cheesecake. I love cheesecake. Just ask my mates at Outsider Tart, in Chiswick, who make the best American cheesecake in London. I'll eat an entire pumpkin pie on my own every 4th July – which is essentially a big cheesecake, isn't it? Really, no? Ok, well, there's no pretending that this is good for your figure, only good for your taste buds.

1 Lightly grease a 20cm springform cake tin with a little sunflower oil.

2 Place the biscuits in a sealable plastic food bag and lightly bash with the end of a wooden spoon to create a fine crumb. Tip into a bowl and mix together with the melted butter and ginger. Tip into the cake tin, pressing down firmly with the back of a spoon, and transfer to the fridge for at least 30 minutes to set.

3 Fill a pan one-third full of water and bring to a simmer, then set a tightly fitting heatproof bowl on top of the pan, making sure the base doesn't touch the water. Break the chocolate into the bowl and allow to melt gently, stirring occasionally. Set aside to cool a little.

4 In a large mixing bowl, beat the double cream until it reaches a thick dropping consistency. Be careful not to over whip it until it's too stiff.

5 In a separate bowl, use a wooden spoon to beat together the cream cheese, icing sugar, lemon zest and cooled chocolate.

6 Gently fold the cream through the cream cheese mixture along with 150g of the raspberries. Lightly crush the raspberries with the back of the spoon when incorporating to get a nice rippled effect. Spoon the mixture over the cheesecake base and smooth over. Allow to set in the fridge for a minimum of 3 hours.

7 Transfer the cheesecake to a large serving plate and scatter the remaining raspberries and the pumpkin seeds over the top to decorate.

VEGAN
PREP TIME: 20 MINUTES
+ 1 HOUR CHILLING
NO COOKING TIME
MAKES 18-20 BALLS

RAW COCONUT, COCOA & ALMOND ENERGY BALLS

200g skin-on almonds
300g dates, pitted and
    roughly chopped
100g dried prunes,
    roughly chopped
3 tbsp crunchy almond
    or peanut butter
3 tbsp coconut butter
1 tsp dark raw cocoa powder
Small pinch of sea salt

Energy balls – that's what they used to call me on building sites because of my balls of energy – and what a treat they are. You'll feel energised after just a couple and they taste good, too. The editor wants me to move on…

Actually, this is an important time to introduce you to raw cocoa powder – all the health shops do it. It's unprocessed, so it's actually good for you and the best chocolate you can use – honest, I own no shares in it!

1 Blitz the almonds in a food processor to create a fine mixture. Set aside 50g of the ground nuts to coat.

2 Add the dates, prunes, nut butter and coconut butter to the 150g of ground almonds and pulse together. Add the cocoa powder and salt, blitzing a couple of times more. Roll the mixture into balls, roughly the size of a ping-pong ball and coat in the chopped almonds. Set aside in the fridge for 1 hour to firm up.

DARK CHOCOLATE & TOASTED HAZELNUT BROWNIES WITH SALTED CARAMEL

200g unsalted butter,
    plus extra for greasing
200g dark chocolate
    (70% cocoa solids),
    roughly chopped
5 medium eggs
200g golden caster sugar
150g soft brown sugar
120g plain wholemeal flour
½ tsp fine sea salt
40g dark raw cocoa powder
80g dark chocolate chunks
100g whole hazelnuts, toasted
    and roughly chopped

FOR THE CARAMEL
130g granulated sugar
20g unsalted butter
6 tbsp double cream
1 vanilla pod, seeds scraped
¼ tsp sea salt flakes

Just pause and read the title again. It says it all. What's not to like? Just make sure you make plenty, because everyone will want one.

1 Preheat the oven to 180°C/fan 160°C/gas 4. Grease a 24 x 20cm baking tin and line it with non-stick baking parchment.

2 Place the butter and chocolate in a medium heatproof bowl and set it neatly over a pan of just-simmering water, making sure the base of the bowl doesn't touch the water. Allow the chocolate and butter to melt together, stirring occasionally, for 5–10 minutes. Set aside and allow to cool down slightly.

3 Meanwhile, make the caramel. In a medium saucepan, place the sugar and 6 tablespoons of water and allow to dissolve over a medium heat. Once the sugar has dissolved, raise the heat and bring to the boil. Do not stir the caramel at any stage, just swirl the pan lightly. Boil rapidly until the caramel is a rich golden brown, then remove from the heat and swirl in the butter. Once the butter has melted, quickly beat in the cream with a whisk and add the vanilla seeds and sea salt flakes.

4 In a large mixing bowl, whisk together the eggs and both sugars using a freestanding mixer or electric hand whisk until fluffy and pale. Into a separate bowl, sift the flour, salt and cocoa powder. Gently fold together the melted chocolate with the sugar and eggs. Add the dry ingredients and again gently fold together, being careful not to knock too much of the air out of the mixture. Stir through the chocolate chunks and half of the nuts. Pour the mixture into the prepared tin. Drizzle the caramel sauce over and ripple it through using a skewer or the sharp tip of a knife. Top the brownie with the remaining hazelnuts and bake in the centre of the oven for 35–40 minutes.

5 Allow to cool down slightly in the tin before slicing into 12 squares. Serve with vanilla ice cream.

VEGETARIAN
PREP TIME: 30 MINUTES
+ 2½ HOURS CHILLING
COOKING TIME: 15 MINUTES
SERVES 8–10

SALTED CARAMEL & MACADAMIA CHEESECAKE

FOR THE CARAMEL
130g granulated sugar
20g unsalted butter
6 tbsp double cream
1 vanilla pod, seeds scraped
¼ tsp sea salt flakes

FOR THE CHEESECAKE
200g coconut biscuits
80g skinned macadamia
  nuts, toasted
60g unsalted butter
150ml double cream
150ml sour cream
500g full-fat cream cheese
40g icing sugar, sifted
30g coconut flakes, toasted

I've mentioned that I love cheesecake – I mean, really love it. If I was locked in a cheesecake factory overnight they'd find an exploded version of me there the next morning. This one's got caramel, too. You're going to make friends with this dessert!

1 In a medium saucepan, dissolve the sugar in 6 tablespoons of water over a medium heat. Once the sugar has dissolved, bring to the boil. Do not stir the caramel, just swirl the pan lightly. Boil rapidly until the caramel is a rich golden brown, then remove from the heat and swirl in the butter. Quickly beat in the cream and add the vanilla seeds and sea salt flakes. Allow the caramel to cool completely at room temperature.

2 Line the bottom of a 24cm springform cake tin with non-stick baking parchment. In a food processor, blitz the coconut biscuits to a fine crumb. Set aside in a large bowl. Blitz half the nuts to a fine crumb and mix with the biscuits and melted butter. Press firmly into the cake tin and set aside in the fridge for 30 minutes to firm up.

3 Whisk the double cream with an electric hand whisk until you have a soft dropping consistency – be careful not to over whip. In a separate bowl, use a wooden spoon to beat together the sour cream, cream cheese and icing sugar. Fold the cream cheese mixture together gently with the cream. Ripple through the cooled-down caramel and spoon into the cake tin. Set aside for 2 hours in the fridge until completely set.

4 Roughly chop the remaining macadamia nuts. Once the cheesecake has chilled, gently release it from its tin, top with the chopped nuts and a good handful of the coconut flakes. Serve sliced into 8–10 wedges.

VEGETARIAN
PREP TIME: 35 MINUTES
COOKING TIME: 30–35 MINUTES
SERVES 6–8

SWEET & SOUR CRUMBLE

300g rhubarb, cut into
    3cm pieces
1 vanilla pod, split lengthways
200g Pink Lady apples,
    peeled and cubed
150g strawberries, halved
2 tbsp maple syrup
Crème fraîche or vanilla
    custard, to serve

FOR THE TOPPING
80g cold salted butter,
    cut into small pieces,
    plus extra for greasing
100g plain flour
125g rolled oats
50g soft brown sugar
50g hazelnuts, roughly chopped
3 tbsp Demerara sugar

This is simply the best crumble in the world. I've added gooseberries before but not everyone likes them, cherries too, but they're fiddly to pip. The topping with oats and crushed hazelnuts is just the bomb, seriously off the scale.

It also works with marg instead of butter and with no flour and no syrup in the fruit – it's about the fruit blend and your taste. Do blanch the rhubarb first so it's not too firm as it cooks slower than other fruit. This is my favourite recipe in the whole book!

1 Preheat the oven to 180°C/fan 160°C/gas 4. Lightly grease a large pie dish and set aside. Place the rhubarb in a medium pan over a low heat with the vanilla pod, cover and gently cook for 5 minutes or until the rhubarb is tender but still holding its shape. Place in the pie dish with the apples, strawberries and maple syrup.

2 In a mixing bowl, rub together the flour and butter with your fingertips until you have a fine crumb. Stir through the oats, sugar and hazelnuts. Top the fruit mixture with the oat crumble and a sprinkle of the Demerara sugar. Place in the oven for 30–35 minutes or until golden brown and bubbling. Serve with a good dollop of crème fraîche or vanilla custard.

KEY LIME PIE

FOR THE PASTRY
250g plain flour,
    plus a little for dusting
50g icing sugar, sifted
A pinch of salt
135g cold butter,
    cut into small cubes
1 medium egg, beaten
1 tbsp ground ginger

FOR THE FILLING
4 medium egg yolks
400g tin condensed milk
Juice of 4 limes and zest of 2

FOR THE JELLY
3 sheets of gelatine
Juice of 5 limes and zest of 1
60ml water
40g caster sugar
1 drop of green food
    colouring

I honestly had my first Key Lime Pie in Key West in the US of A where it was invented, and very lovely it was, too. Obviously you need to like lime, otherwise try Key Lemon Pie, or I wonder if Key Orange would work? I don't see why not. Right, I'm off to the kitchen to find out...

1 Pulse the flour, icing sugar, salt and butter in a food processor until the mixture resembles breadcrumbs. Add the beaten egg and 2–3 tablespoons of cold water or milk. Pulse until the mixture just comes together to form a dough, adding a tiny bit more cold water if needed. Wrap in cling film and chill for 30 minutes.

2 Roll out the pastry on a lightly floured work surface to the thickness of a £1 coin and use it line a deep, 23cm loose-bottomed tart tin, making sure the edge of the pastry stands just a little proud of the rim. Trim the edges, then prick the base with a fork and return it to the fridge to chill for a further 30 minutes. Don't be tempted to skip this step – it will help prevent any shrinkage.

3 Preheat the oven to 200°C/fan 180°C/gas 6 and put a baking sheet in the oven to heat up. Remove the pastry case from the fridge, line it with baking parchment and fill it with baking beans. Bake in the oven for 20 minutes, then remove the parchment and the beans and return to the oven for a further 5 minutes. Set aside. Reduce the oven to 180°C/fan 160°C/gas 4.

Recipe continued overleaf

Recipe continued

4 Meanwhile, start on the filling. Beat the egg yolks in a large bowl with an electric hand whisk for 3 minutes. Add the condensed milk and continue to whisk for a couple of minutes. Finally, whisk in the lime juice and zest. Spoon the mixture over the biscuit base, swirling it with the back of a spoon to cover evenly. Place in the oven and bake for 15–20 minutes, until just set. Remove from the oven and allow to cool completely, then remove from the tin and chill in the fridge.

5 For the lime jelly, soak the gelatine sheets in enough cold water to cover for 5 minutes. Put the lime juice, 60ml water and the sugar into a pan and slowly bring almost to the boil, dissolving the sugar. Remove from the heat. Squeeze the excess water from the gelatine leaves and add to the pan, stirring to dissolve. Add the lime zest and food colouring, stir, then transfer to a jug and leave to cool for 30 minutes.

6 Pour the jelly over the pie, stopping once the case is full. Return it to the fridge for 1 hour to set. Serve in slices.

VEGETARIAN
PREP TIME: 20 MINUTES
COOKING TIME: 1 HOUR 15 MINUTES
MAKES 1 X 18CM CAKE

SWEET APPLE & ALMOND CAKE

115g butter, melted,
  plus extra for greasing
225g self-raising flour
1 tsp baking powder
170g caster sugar
1 tsp almond extract
2 medium eggs
400g Braeburn apples, cored
  and each chopped into 8
25g flaked almonds
4 tbsp apricot jam, warmed

Almonds are almonds – better toasted than not, I always think, but there's only so far you can be bothered when you're starting out. Sweet apple is potentially the best fruit for dessert in the world; we Brits don't see it because it's so common, but think about it, in the US apple pie has legendary status, ask a French pastry chef about tarte Tatin and he'll go misty eyed, or ask an Austrian about strudel and he'll start slapping his lederhosen.

1 Preheat the oven to 160°C/fan 140°C/gas 3. Grease an 18cm round cake tin and line the base with non-stick baking parchment.

2 Empty the flour, baking powder and caster sugar into a large bowl and pour in the melted butter and almond extract. Stir to combine, then add the eggs, one at a time, mixing well after each addition.

3 Spoon half of the cake mixture into the cake tin before dropping two-thirds of the apples over in the centre. Blob over the remaining mixture and drop over the remaining apple pieces. Sprinkle with the almonds.

4 Bake on the centre shelf of the oven for about 1 hour–1 hour 15 minutes or until the cake is golden, firm to the touch and slightly pulled away from the sides of the tin. Allow to cool for a good 10 minutes before removing from the tin and brushing with warmed apricot jam.

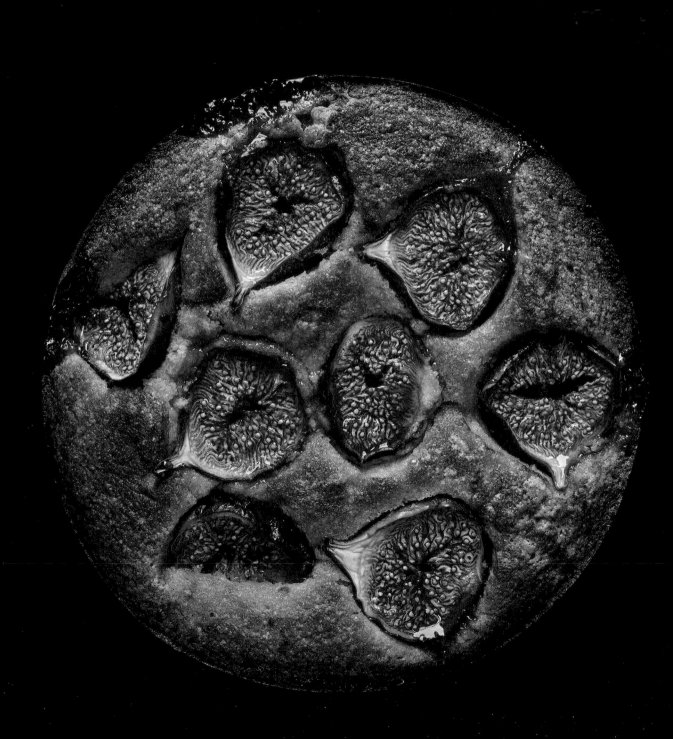

STICKY FIG & ALMOND CAKE

250g unsalted butter, softened, plus extra for greasing
125g soft brown sugar
125g caster sugar
3 large eggs, lightly beaten
200g ground almonds
100g plain flour
½ tsp fine salt
Zest of 1 large orange and 1 tsp of the juice
Seeds of 1 vanilla pod
70ml buttermilk
4 large figs, cut in halves
1 tbsp runny honey
30g whole almonds, roughly chopped
Crème fraîche or ginger ice cream, to serve

This has got fruit in it so it must be good for you. Who am I trying to kid? It just tastes really good, is easy to make and everyone needs a treat once in a while.

1 Preheat the oven to 180°C/fan 160°C/gas 4. Butter a 20cm springform cake tin and line with non-stick baking parchment.

2 In a large mixing bowl, beat together the butter and both types of sugar until doubled in volume and pale. Beat in the eggs in several additions, making sure they are well incorporated after each addition. Fold in the almonds, flour and salt followed by the orange zest and vanilla seeds. Stir through the buttermilk.

3 Pour the cake mix into the tin, smooth the top gently and arrange the fig halves over, then finish with a drizzle of the orange juice on each fig. Bake in the centre of the oven for 45–50 minutes or until a skewer inserted into the centre comes out clean.

4 While still hot, brush the cake gently with the runny honey. Allow to cool in the tin for 15 minutes before carefully removing from the tin and scattering over the chopped almonds.

5 Serve the cake in wedges, warm or cold, with a generous dollop of thick crème fraîche or a scoop of ginger ice cream.

WHOLE ORANGE & ALMOND PUDDING CAKE

Butter, for greasing
2 small oranges (approx. 375g)
6 medium eggs
250g caster sugar
250g ground almonds
1 tsp baking powder
½ tsp ground cloves
30g flaked almonds, toasted
Zest of 1 orange

TO SERVE
Icing sugar
Crème fraîche

It's a pudding and a cake – a cake and pudding – what's not to get excited about? I recommend eating it warmed up and with a dollop of vegan cashew-based ice cream.

1 Preheat the oven to 190°C/fan 170°C/gas 5. Grease a 22cm springform tin and line with baking parchment.

2 Put the whole oranges in a large pan and cover with cold water, then bring to the boil and cook for 2 hours until soft. Drain and leave to cool. Once cool, cut the oranges in half and remove the pips. Put the oranges – skins, pith, fruit and all – in a food processor and give them a quick blitz.

3 Gently beat the eggs by hand, adding the caster sugar, almonds, baking powder and ground cloves. Mix well before stirring through the pulped oranges.

4 Pour the cake mixture into the tin, scatter with the almonds and orange zest and bake for 1 hour–1 hour 15 minutes, until the top is golden and a skewer inserted in the centre of the cake comes out clean.

5 Remove from the oven and leave to cool on a wire rack, but still in the tin. When the cake is cold, remove from the tin. Dust with icing sugar and serve alongside dollops of crème fraîche.

VEGAN
PREP TIME: 40 MINUTES
+ 3 HOURS CHILLING
COOKING TIME: 5 MINUTES
MAKES 12 SQUARES

VEGAN AVOCADO MILLIONAIRE'S SHORTBREAD

2 tbsp coconut oil, plus
    extra for greasing
80g pecan nuts
100g cashew nuts
50g desiccated coconut
50g pitted Medjool dates,
    roughly chopped

FOR THE CARAMEL
250g pitted Medjool dates
125ml unsweetened
    almond milk
25ml maple syrup
150ml coconut oil
Pinch of salt
1 tsp vanilla extract

**FOR THE CHOCOLATE
TOPPING**
1 large ripe avocado,
    peeled and stoned
80g vegan dark chocolate,
    melted
3 tbsp maple syrup

I know, I know, with avocado? Are you having a laugh? Seriously, some of the best ice cream of any kind that I've ever tasted is vegan and made with creamed cashews. So don't judge, just go with the shortbread made with avocado.

1 Lightly oil a non stick 20cm square brownie tin and line with baking parchment. Place the pecan nuts, cashews and coconut into a food processor and blitz until you have a fine crumb. Add the dates and coconut oil and blitz several times to create a dense, thick paste. Tip the mixture into the tin and press down firmly with the back of a spoon to create a compact base. Chill in the fridge for 20 minutes.

2 For the caramel, add the dates, almond milk, maple syrup and coconut oil to a saucepan with a generous pinch of salt and bring to the boil for 2–3 minutes until the dates are really soft, then tip into a blender, add the vanilla extract and blitz to a smooth purée. Add a little more salt to taste. Pour over the base and spread to the sides of the tin, making it as smooth as possible. Chill in the fridge while you prepare the final layer.

3 Use an electric hand whisk to beat together the avocado, melted dark chocolate and maple syrup. Spread the mixture over the cool caramel layer, smoothing over with a palette knife, and chill in the fridge for 2–2½ hours until set. Cut into 12 squares and eat immediately or store in the fridge.

RICH VEGAN CHOCOLATE SPREAD

250g hazelnuts, skinned
100g vegan dark
    chocolate, melted
100g icing sugar
3 tbsp cocoa powder

This is ridiculously lovely and if it ever leaves the bowl without you eating it simply with a spoon I'll be amazed. Remember, raw chocolate is better for you, so try to substitute raw cocoa powder from your deli for the cocoa powder. The kids will go ape for this as a treat.

1 Heat the hazelnuts in a dry frying pan over a medium–high heat for 5 minutes until they are very lightly browned. While they are still hot, tip the toasted hazelnuts into a food processor and process until you have a creamy paste. This will take 4–5 minutes, so be patient!

2 Add the melted chocolate, icing sugar and cocoa powder and blend until the mixture is combined and has become a paste. Scrape into a jar and enjoy spread on toast. This will keep for up to a month, if stored in a sealed jar in the fridge.

APRICOT & WALNUT FRIDGE BARS

2 tbsp coconut oil, plus extra for greasing
100g walnuts, roughly chopped
80g pitted dates, roughly chopped
80g dried apricots, chopped
75g smooth peanut or any other nut butter
2 tbsp dark raw cocoa powder
½ tsp salt
3 tbsp maple syrup
Zest of 1 large orange
50g puffed rice
50g rolled oats
40g dark chocolate chips

Make 'em.

Save 'em.

Take 'em to work.

Eat them in front of your mates, saying, 'Mmm, I made these. Sorry, I've only got the one.'

1 Grease a 23cm square brownie tin and line with non-stick baking parchment.

2 Place half the walnuts in a food processor and blitz until you have a fine crumb. Throw in the dates, apricots and the nut butter, cocoa powder, coconut oil, salt, maple syrup and orange zest, blitzing until you have a thick smooth mixture.

3 Transfer to a bowl and combine the mixture with the remaining walnuts, puffed rice, oats and chocolate chips. Spoon into the prepared tin, smoothing over and pressing down firmly with the back of a spoon. Place in the fridge to chill and firm up for 3–4 hours. Once chilled, slice into 12 chunky bars. These bars are best eaten straight from the fridge – do not allow them to warm up too much!

VEGETARIAN
PREP TIME: 20 MINUTES
COOKING TIME: 45 MINUTES
MAKES 1 LOAF CAKE

BLUEBERRY, BANANA & ALMOND LOAF

100g unsalted butter,
   plus extra for greasing
100g caster sugar
1 ripe banana, mashed
2 medium eggs
100g ground almonds
90g fine polenta
1 tsp baking powder
100ml natural yoghurt
100g blueberries

FOR THE SYRUP
Juice of 1 large lemon
50g caster sugar

Many years ago I stayed in a friend's house in St Vincent. Oh, I know, international playboy me! Actually, he let me have it for free as it wasn't anywhere posh and a tax rebate took care of the flights. Anyway… there was a shack I went to every morning for coffee as thick and dark as creosote and banana bread. I've pinged in blueberries here so that it's now my recipe not theirs. Talk to my lawyers…

1 Preheat the oven to 180°C/fan 160°C/gas 4. Grease a 900g loaf tin and line with non-stick baking parchment.

2 Using an electric hand mixer, cream the butter and sugar together in a bowl until soft and pale. Stir through the mashed banana. Beat in the eggs, one at a time, adding half of the ground almonds with each egg. Stir through the polenta, baking powder, yoghurt and half of the blueberries.

3 Pour the batter into the loaf tin and sprinkle the remaining blueberries over the top. Bake for about 45 minutes or until a skewer inserted into the centre comes out clean.

4 Meanwhile, make a syrup by simply warming the lemon juice, sugar and 1 tablespoon of water in a small pan.

5 As soon as the cake is cooked, remove from the oven and immediately pour the syrup over it while still in the tin. Don't worry if the syrup collects in the corners slightly; it will soak into the sponge. Allow to cool before removing from the tin and serving cut into slices.

VEGETARIAN
PREP TIME: 15 MINUTES
+ OVERNIGHT FREEZING
COOKING TIME: 5 MINUTES
SERVES 6–8

NO-CHURN PECAN PIE ICE CREAM

397g tin condensed milk
2 tbsp maple syrup
1 tsp vanilla paste or extract
1½ tsp ground cinnamon
750ml double cream
100g pecan nuts,
   roughly chopped
4 shortbread biscuits, broken

Yes, you can make your own ice cream! This is a veggie-only one and hugely indulgent but – what the hell – you're eating so healthy these days you can afford a blow out or a day off. Vegan cream doesn't really work so well here but I'm working on it. Next book, maybe!

1 Mix together the condensed milk, maple syrup, vanilla and cinnamon in a large bowl until combined.

2 In a separate bowl, lightly whisk the cream until you have a soft dropping consistency.

3 In a small frying pan over a medium heat, gently toast the pecans for about 5 minutes or until lightly browned. Leave to cool a little.

4 Keeping a little of the pecans and biscuits to one side, gently fold the cream into the condensed milk mixture along with the chopped toasted nuts and broken biscuits. Spoon into a freezerproof container, sprinkle with the remaining biscuits and pecans, cover and freeze overnight. Pull out of the freezer 10 minutes before serving to soften slightly, and scoop into glasses or bowls.

VEGETARIAN
PREP TIME: 30 MINUTES
+ OVERNIGHT CHILLING
COOKING TIME: 25 MINUTES
MAKES 12 CAKES

CHOCOLATE CUPCAKES WITH CASHEW FROSTING

270ml hazelnut milk
1 tbsp rice vinegar
100ml sunflower oil
150g Demerara sugar
250g self-raising flour
70g dark raw cocoa powder
¼ tsp salt
½ tsp bicarbonate of soda

FOR THE FROSTING
250g raw unsalted cashew nuts
150ml coconut oil, melted
½ tbsp rice vinegar
110ml maple syrup
¼ tsp salt
1 tsp vanilla essence

Here's another easy recipe from my restaurant in Shrewsbury. The customers love them.

1 First, make the frosting. Place the cashew nuts, coconut oil, 150ml water, vinegar, syrup, salt and vanilla in the food processor and blitz for 5–10 minutes. Transfer to a bowl, cover with cling film and chill overnight.

2 Preheat the oven to 200°C/fan 180°C/gas 6. Line a 12-hole cupcake tray with paper cases.

3 Empty the nut milk, vinegar, oil and sugar into a small saucepan and place on a medium–low heat for 4–5 minutes, stirring constantly until the sugar has just dissolved. Remove from the heat and allow it to cool slightly.

4 Sift the flour, cocoa powder, salt and bicarbonate of soda into a large bowl and gradually pour over the almond milk mixture. Combine quickly into a wet cake mixture. Spoon into the cake cases and bake for 15–18 minutes until baked through and springy to the touch.

5 Remove the frosting from the fridge 10–15 minutes before you want to use it and leave at room temperature to soften slightly. Scoop it into a piping bag and pipe over the cupcakes, or use the back of a spoon to smooth the icing on.

INDEX

ACKNOWLEDGEMENTS
Thanks to Lisa and Charlotte
for helping me through my
first publishing steps. Georgina
who is dedicated and wonderful
and Sammy Jo for getting me
started. My true friend and life
guide Hilary and lovely Jane
for seeing possibilities and
believing. My Charlotte who
everyone loves. And thanks
finally to Larry, who knows
me so well and is the most
steadfast of friends.